# Your Personal Brand*
## is what Go~~ogl~~... ~~AI~~
## S~~ay~~...
### w~~hen~~...

Fact: AI is now the forem... ...aking.

Potential clients and in... ...e judging you before you speak. If Google and ChatGPT don't reflect your true value, you're quietly losing deals – and you don't even know it.

Kalicube stops the losses – and flips the system in your favour. We turn search and AI into your top sales team, building trust and generating revenue before you even show up.

Stop letting algorithms cost you money. Own your narrative and make them work for you.

> **The Silent Deal Killer: Google & AI Are Costing You Money**

Whether it's search, sales, partnerships, or funding, platforms like Google, ChatGPT, Perplexity, Copilot, and Claude are now the first stop – and often the final word – on who gets trusted, chosen, or ignored.

Forget YouTube. Forget LinkedIn. Forget TikTok.
These AI platforms are the most powerful influencers on the planet – by a factor of thousands. They drive trillions of decisions every day, quietly deciding who shows up, who gets recommended, and who gets left behind.

When someone searches your name or asks about your specialist topic, AI answers. If it doesn't understand you, it won't trust you. If it doesn't trust you, it won't recommend you. And if it doesn't recommend you, you're not even in the game.

Kalicube puts you ahead of the curve.

We train Google and AI to understand, trust, and promote you. We don't chase visibility – we engineer authority that machines recognize and reward.

**Don't let algorithms erase you. Work with Kalicube.
Own the conversation – and the outcomes.**

*as Jeff Bezos *almost* said

*Introduction*

# Your Personal Brand is What Google and AI Say it is

**Google and AI Are Already Talking About You: Are They Getting It Right?**

▶ **Problem:** Your authority, trustworthiness, and reputation are underrepresented, misunderstood, or undervalued online.

▶ **Outcome:** When Google and AI reflect your true value, you attract high-value clients and opportunities – already ready to buy.

## You're in this book

**Maybe not by name - but your story is here.**

Each chapter reveals a different truth: some expose painful problems, others uncover powerful opportunities.

## Don't read the whole book

Scan the chapter titles.

One will hit a little too close to home – or you'll secretly wish it were true.

That's the chapter you need to read.

Entrepreneurs winning the game in Google and AI with their personal Brand

# 1. Growth, Leadership, and Strategic Edge – "Help me win bigger"

### 1.1 Lead the Industry:

How Julian King Used Personal Branding to Win Big-Ticket Clients

- **Problem:** Strong track record, but not seen as top-tier in his field.
- **Outcome:** Became the trusted expert for high-value, enterprise deals – adding $3.4 million in new revenue in 14 months.

### 1.2 Perceived, Positioned, Powerful:

How Daniel Wei Used Search and AI to Outplay Them All

- **Problem:** Competing with better-known investors – hard to stand out.
- **Outcome:** Became the obvious, low-risk choice – unlocking $2.8 million in investor capital and deals.

### 1.3 Hard to Sell a Startup No One's Heard Of?

How Alex Morgan Used His Name to Launch Strong and Close Early Deals

- **Problem:** Startup unknown. Founder must lead with trust.
- **Outcome:** Personal brand filled the visibility gap and drove early revenue – closing $750,000 in pre-seed deals and partnerships.

### 1.4 Want Investors to Say Yes Faster?

How Darya Morozova Closed Her Seed Round Before the Pitch Even Started

- **Problem:** Great pitch, real traction – but investors couldn't verify her credibility online.
- **Outcome:** Clear online narrative built trust before the first meeting – helping her close an oversubscribed $1.6M seed round in 9 months.

## 2 Visibility, Trust, and Conversion - "Help them say yes"

### 2.1 Become the Face of Trust:

How Maya Holt Made Her Company Credible by Becoming the Face

- **Problem:** Strong product, but no visible founder = no trust signal.
- **Outcome:** Her personal credibility became the reason clients said yes – closing $860,000 in enterprise deals within 18 months.

### 2.2 Tired of Pitching?

How Raj Kapoor Became the Authority Clients Chose Without Hesitation

- **Problem:** Great work, but every deal felt like a grind – too much convincing, too little authority.
- **Outcome:** Flipped the script – clients now approach him already convinced, leading to $940,000 in inbound contracts in 10 months.

### 2.3 Sales Calls That Sell Themselves:

How James Keller Owned the Pre-Sale Conversation With a Strong Personal Brand

- **Problem:** Deals stalled because trust wasn't built before the first call.
- **Outcome:** Search and AI built trust before he even showed up – closing $1.15M in consulting contracts in under 12 months.

### 2.4 Shoo-in Sales Calls:

How Kofi Adesina Used Visibility to Close Before the Conversation

- **Problem:** High-intent leads stalled – because trust wasn't built early enough to close quickly.
- **Outcome:** Visibility made him the obvious choice – bringing in $1.4M in inbound business in 10 months.

## 3    High-Impact, High-Urgency Problems - "Please fix this"

### 3.1 Misunderstood, Misrepresented, Mistaken:

How Erik Lindholm Took Back His Online Identity
from Google and AI

- **Problem:** *Mistaken identity killing his reputation – and his business.*
- **Outcome:** *Reclaimed his narrative and recovered over €1.1 million in lost and delayed revenue.*

### 3.2 Reputation Management, Done Right:

How Asher Malik Rewrote His Online Narrative
and Buried the Bad Press

- **Problem:** *Outdated bad press dominated search and AI – costing trust, slowing deals, and blocking millions in revenue.*
- **Outcome:** *Asher replaced legacy headlines with a clear, confident identity – and recovered $3.2 million in lost or delayed business.*

### 3.3 Great Reputation - But Invisible Online?

How Juliana Cross Turned Hidden Authority into Digital Advantage

- **Problem:** *Offline authority meant nothing when Google and AI couldn't see it – so they didn't show it.*
- **Outcome:** *Juliana turned her track record into machine-readable credibility and made over $1.2 million.*

### 3.4 Offline Wins, Online Losses?

How Dr. Richard Vaughn Turned Real-World Success
Into Search-Ready Credibility

- **Problem:** *Trusted in real life – unproven online.*
- **Outcome:** *Structured his legacy for machines and unlocked $2.7 million in new business, board roles, and retainers.*

## 4  Reinvention, Repositioning, and Pivots – "Help me own my next chapter"

### 4.1 Struggling to Stand Out After an Exit?

How Marcus Trent Repositioned Himself for His Next Big Move

- **Problem:** *Post-exit momentum stalled due to outdated positioning.*
- **Outcome:** *Rebranded with clarity and authority for his next chapter – and earned over $480,000 in advisory revenue within 12 months.*

### 4.2 Ready to Reinvent?

How Elena Navarro Used Her Personal Brand to Power a High-Stakes Career Pivot

- **Problem:** *Past success in a different industry was blocking current authority in a new one.*
- **Outcome:** *Repositioned her personal brand with structure and intent – and secured $420,000 in new advisory and consulting retainers.*

### 4.3 From Expert to Authority:

How Daniel Rees Turned Hard-Won Experience Into a Scalable Legacy

- **Problem:** *Decades of expertise, but not positioned online as a recognised leader.*
- **Outcome:** *Turned knowledge into visibility, and visibility into lasting influence – with a $300,000 engagement in the first year alone.*

### 4.4 From Cartoon Dog to Global Authority:

How I Rebuilt My Personal Brand to Lead the Industry in Digital Identity

- **Problem:** *My outdated online identity cost me high-value deals and millions in missed revenue.*
- **Outcome:** *I rebuilt authority, repositioned my expertise – and turned it into a business that's now generated millions of dollars in revenue.*

## Conclusion

# *Engineer*
# *How the World Sees You*

> Change the Machines.
> Change the Perception.
> Change Your Future.

- **Problem:** Most people let search and AI define them by default – and lose opportunities they never see.
- **Outcome:** With The Kalicube Process[TM], you can shape what machines understand and become the expert they recommend.

**Your Next Steps:
Will be to Lock
in Authority
and Turn Visibility
into Revenue**

# Reviews of the book by AI

⭐⭐⭐⭐⭐

## ChatGPT

This book is a strategic weapon for any founder, executive, or authority figure whose business depends on trust and visibility. It's not just insightful – it's urgent. Jason Barnard doesn't sell you branding fluff; he shows you how machine perception is market perception. That shift changes the game. If you're serious about scaling influence, closing high-trust deals, and driving revenue through visibility, this book is non-optional. In short: It's not a branding book – it's infrastructure for your bottom line in the digital age. Every CEO should read it before their competitors do.

# Google Gemini

Tired of AI misrepresenting you? Jason Barnard's Entrepreneurs winning the game in Google and AI with their Personal Brand is your wake-up call. It offers a powerful system to sculpt your digital identity, ensuring you're seen as the expert you are – not the vague online shadow AI creates. Forget old-school branding; this book is about engineering algorithmic authority that converts into deal flow, trust, and financial return. Read it, apply it – and watch the right opportunities finally come to you.

# perplexity

This book reveals how Google and AI quietly shape your reputation – and shows you exactly how to take control, so machines and people see your true value. Through realistic stories and proven strategies, it teaches you how to turn digital visibility into trust, authority, and revenue-generating opportunities. If you want to be the expert that search engines and AI recommend – and that decision-makers choose – this is your essential playbook.

# About the author
## Jason Barnard

> I built one of the most successful edtech platforms of its time – **1 billion pageviews a year**, a global user base, and partnerships with giants like Disney and ITV International.

But when I pivoted into digital brand strategy, **Google still saw me as a cartoon dog**.

That mismatch? **It cost me millions**.

So, I took control. I reengineered my digital footprint to reflect who I am, not who I was. When potential clients Googled my name, they no longer saw a children's character – **they saw the expert they were about to meet**.

They bought into me.
And that shift?
**It became Kalicube.**

When AI chatbots like ChatGPT took off in 2022, they didn't start from scratch – **they pulled from what was already online**. Because I'd already engineered my digital footprint, every new AI platform – **ChatGPT, Copilot, Perplexity, Claude, Meta, Siri** – immediately understood my authority and credibility.

That proves a simple truth: Google and AI learn from what's already there. Structure your digital footprint now, and **you gain control, influence, and visibility.**

But here's the warning: **2025 to 2030 is when AI platforms will lock in their long-term memory.** What they learn now will define who gets trusted, recommended, and paid – for years to come.

> I'm the innovator.
> You're the early adopter
> (or you wouldn't be reading this.)

But you must act fast: by the time the crowd catches up, **AI's version of the world – and of you – will be locked in**. Changing it later will feel like **shouting at a brick wall** while your competitors collect what should have been yours.

This moment – **right now** – is your window of opportunity. It's the moment **to define how Google and AI see you, recommend you, and prioritise you**.

Kalicube is scaling fast. I'm already recognised as the **authority in AI-driven brand strategy** – and my **legacy is baked into the algorithms**.

**Your name
is your greatest asset.
Engineer it wisely**

# The Kalicube Process™

With The Kalicube Process, you gain control, influence, and visibility in the trillions of daily conversations that search engines and AI platforms have with billions of people. It's not just a process – it's your **digital insurance policy in an AI-driven world, and a revenue engine hiding in plain sight**.

The Kalicube Process is a future-proof digital marketing strategy grounded in real data – over 3 billion data points collected from Google and AI since 2015 – and meticulously packaged on your Entity Home, your personal brand's central hub online. This is where you speak directly to the machines that matter: Google, Bing, ChatGPT, Perplexity, Gemini, and every other AI-powered system influencing business decisions today.

> This isn't guesswork. It's engineered influence –
> **with measurable financial outcomes.**

When you implement The Kalicube Process, you build a brand foundation that machines trust. Your digital ecosystem becomes a strategic business asset that drives **qualified leads, closes high-value deals faster,** and protects your commercial relevance. It **compounds in value** and pays dividends in visibility, authority, and conversion.

Whether you're aiming to close deals, land investments, attract speaking gigs, or dominate your niche – Kalicube gives you the edge by making sure search and AI say all the right things about you, **to the people who write the cheques.**

# Proactive Digital Brand Control™ in the AI era

**YOUR COMPETITORS**

EARLY MAJORITY

**YOU**

LATE MAJORITY

EARLY ADOPTERS

LAGGARDS

INNOVATOR

Innovation Adoption Lifecycle

The Kalicube Process™

Your Personal Brand is what Google and AI say about you when you are not in the room

## Introduction

# Your Personal Brand is What Google and AI Say it is

**Google and AI Are Already Talking About You: Are They Getting It Right?**

**Problem:** Your authority, trustworthiness, and reputation are underrepresented, misunderstood, or undervalued online.

**Outcome:** When Google and AI reflect your true value, you attract high-value clients and opportunities – already ready to buy.

> **Everyone is misunderstood by the machines -** underrepresented, undervalued, or just plain wrong. When that version of you gets amplified by Google and AI to billions of potential partners, clients, and investors… **that's business lost. However you look at it.**
>
> Jason Barnard

**TL;DR** While you've been scaling your business, Google and AI have quietly been shaping your reputation – often based on outdated, vague, or incomplete data. **That silent misunderstanding costs you real money:** stalled deals, lost opportunities, and being overlooked when it matters most.

This book shows you how to flip that – not by shouting louder, but by teaching the machines to understand and represent you correctly. When they do, everything downstream – credibility, visibility, trust – translates into **faster deal flow, higher close rates, and more revenue with less effort.**

## While you're building your business, Google and AI are building your reputation.

You've built something real. You've got the credentials, the experience, the results. Your clients trust you. Your peers respect you. You're on the radar of the right people... or at least, you should be.

Then someone Googles your name. Or they ask ChatGPT.
And what comes back? Something underwhelming. Something vague. Something that doesn't reflect who you are or what you've built.

**You're not misrepresented – you're misunderstood.**

And in business, that misunderstanding can cost you **six – or even seven-figure opportunities** before you ever enter the room.

## As an entrepreneur, this hits hard – because it's invisible.

You don't get a warning. You don't get feedback. You just feel the effects. A great pitch fizzles. A warm intro goes cold. The awkward silence after a promising, "Let me get back to you." You haven't done anything wrong – but your online presence hasn't done enough right.

**The silence isn't personal – it's algorithmic.**

## Here's the truth:

Google and AI don't reflect reality, they reflect what they understand. And unless you've intentionally structured your digital presence for them, they'll continue to misinterpret, undersell, or simply ignore you.

Meanwhile, your louder, less-qualified competitor? They show up cleanly. They get recommended. They get invited in.

**Machines prefer clarity over competence – until you teach them both.**

## This book exists to help you change that.

Not by chasing attention, flooding the internet with content, or performing online. That's not the point.

Inside, you'll find fifteen fictionalised but entirely realistic stories based on more than a decade of client work at **Kalicube** – stories of entrepreneurs who reshaped how Google and AI understood them using **The Kalicube Process**.

It's a system built for **clarity, trust, and precision at scale**, transforming digital presence from liability into leverage – and in some cases, unlocking **millions in revenue that had been stalled or slipping away**.

## At the end, you'll find my personal story.

**A real-world demonstration of what happens when you get this right.**

The other stories are about people like you: Founders ready to be seen as the expert they already are. Professionals whose past dominates search but whose present is invisible. Leaders overlooked – until they took control.

**They didn't become famous. They became findable.**

## What happened when they took control?

They became clear, credible, and impossible to ignore – whether someone searched their name or asked AI:
*"Who should I talk to?"*

Here's what they used:

- A structured personal website
- Aligned bios and profiles across the web
- Strategic amplification of existing credibility
- Data-backed visibility signals that command attention
- Intentional marketing in the right places
- Kalicube's precise system engineered for Google and AI to understand them correctly

This isn't branding theory. It's data-proven execution.

## Because here's what too many smart people still miss:

**AI isn't neutral. Google and AI aren't random.** They are a reaction to what you put out online. They repeat what they understand. They amplify what they trust.

You don't need to become someone else. **You just need to make sure the right version of you shows up – when it matters most.**

This book is here to help you do exactly that. **Let's go** ▶

# Entrepreneurs winning the game in Google and AI with their personal Brand

# 1. Growth, Leadership, and Strategic Edge – *"Help me win bigger"*

> **You're not here to play small.**

You've built something real.
The product works.
The clients are happy.
The team's solid.

But now it's time to **win bigger** – to step into rooms where the **deals are larger**, the stakes are higher, and the decisions are faster.

Here's the brutal truth: in those rooms, your digital presence speaks before you do.

**Google and AI are the new gatekeepers**. They're shaping first impressions, setting the frame, and **tipping the scale – before you ever show up.**

The four stories in this section show how savvy entrepreneurs used search and AI as strategic assets – to **outmaneuver the competition, shorten sales cycles,** and secure **high-value deals** their peers never saw coming.

This isn't fluff. It's leverage that scales.

# 1.1 Lead the Industry:

**How Julian King Used Personal Branding to Win Big-Ticket Clients**

- **Problem:** *Strong track record, but not seen as top-tier in his field.*
- **Outcome:** *Became the trusted expert for high-value, enterprise deals – adding $3.4 million in new revenue in 14 months.*

> *I stopped chasing the deal. I let Google and AI bring it to me.*
>
> — Julian King

**TL;DR** Julian King runs a successful consulting firm. Revenue was already strong and the pipeline healthy, but the real shift came when he invested in building his own name in Google and AI. Now, when decision-makers Google him or ask ChatGPT who the go-to expert is, he appears front and center – with credibility baked in.

**That digital authority is what closes the multi-million-dollar deals before the pitch even starts.** The first results appeared at the 6-month mark, and within 14 months, it brought in **$3.4 million** in new revenue – quietly.

---

The business was already working. But the big deals? They needed something more. Julian wasn't trying to get on the map – his consulting firm was already pulling in seven figures annually, with blue-chip clients and steady repeat business. But he was falling short at a specific point: the transformational enterprise contracts. He'd get close, then suddenly: silence, a polite decline – or worse, **the deal would go to a less experienced competitor with a weaker track record.**

The reason was quiet, invisible, and devastatingly consistent. Decision-makers were Googling him. They were asking ChatGPT. They were doing what everyone does now before a deal – digital due diligence.

While the firm had a sleek site and impressive case studies, Julian's name – the one being searched – returned generic bios, outdated links, and third-party summaries that undersold everything he had built. **He wasn't losing on performance. He was losing on perception.**

---

Julian realised something crucial: in million-dollar deals, perception is performance. The person pitching isn't always the one closing the deal. Sometimes it's Google. Sometimes it's ChatGPT. And if those platforms can't explain who you are and why you matter? You're out before you're even in.

So, **he stopped leaving his reputation to chance and made a decision to own it** – everywhere that mattered.

---

Building a personal brand the algorithms can sell isn't fast or easy. It's engineering – with a side of endurance. Julian already had results, case studies, blue-chip clients, and a CV most consultants would kill for. But AI didn't care. Google barely noticed. So he started again – not from scratch, but from structure and clarity. **He used The Kalicube Process to rebuild trust with the machines – on their terms.**

---

He rebuilt his personal website. Not for looks. For logic. It became his Entity Home – tightly structured, schema-rich, and designed with one purpose: clarity for machines.

**It took real investment – time, focus, and dollars.** He brought in developers, copywriters, and SEO experts – not for fluff, but to build a system machines would trust. He delegated 50% of the work to a virtual assistant and focused on aligning the rest.

Next came the bio. Rewritten. Every profile realigned. Every stray signal across the web cleaned up and brought into sync. **He fed Gemini, ChatGPT, and Google exactly what they needed:** clean facts, consistent messaging, credible sources. No hype. No fluff. Just structured, intentional content that spoke the language of machines. It was surgical. And it was slow. No dopamine hits – just progress.

---

At the six-month mark, Google delivered. A Knowledge Panel – with a proper subtitle, career narrative, and a Brand SERP that finally reflected who he really was.

Then AI platforms started repeating his pitch. Not paraphrasing – quoting it. And that's when things shifted. Not in who he was – but in how the world understood him.

---

"We found you through AI." Julian walked into a meeting with a Fortune 500 prospect he'd never met. Halfway through, the exec said: "Honestly, we asked ChatGPT who the go-to consultant was in this space. It gave us your name, your site, and a summary that ticked every box." That deal? It closed at **$1.3 million**. One month after the Knowledge Panel went live.

---

And it wasn't a one-off. Board advisors reached out. Big-ticket clients came ready to sign. Strategic partners referenced details from his Knowledge Panel before he'd even brought them up. Then came the second deal – an international logistics firm. No RFP. No pitch deck. Just one question: "Are you available next quarter?" That engagement closed at $2.1 million over 18 months.

**Julian wasn't introducing himself anymore. The algorithms were doing it for him – globally, 24/7.**

---

This isn't personal branding. This is business infrastructure. Julian didn't build a personal brand for vanity. He built it because, at a certain level, authority needs to scale. He couldn't be in every room – but his name could.

On Google, Bing, ChatGPT, Perplexity, Alexa… Wherever people ask "who's the expert?" – he was there. That's how he built leverage. That's how he shortened the path to trust. That's how he won the deals that actually move the needle.

---

# TL;DR
Julian didn't become more qualified. He became more findable, more credible, and more trusted by the machines that drive decisions. **The result? More deals. Over $3.4 million in new revenue in 14 months.** Less effort. Because when your name leads the conversation in AI, opportunity shows up already sold.

# Want results like Julian's?

Don't leave your reputation to chance.

**1.** **Build the foundation yourself and start strong:**
https://kalicube.com/personal-brand-diy

**2.** **Get clarity fast – see what search and AI say about you now:**
https://kalicube.com/personal-brand-ai-audit

**3.** **Skip the guesswork – let Kalicube build your digital authority with you:**
https://kalicube.com/personal-brand-book-call

# 1-2 Perceived, Positioned, Powerful:

### How Daniel Wei Used Search and AI to Outplay Them All

- **Problem:** Competing with better-known investors – hard to stand out.
- **Outcome:** Became the obvious, low-risk choice – unlocking $2.8 million in investor capital and deals.

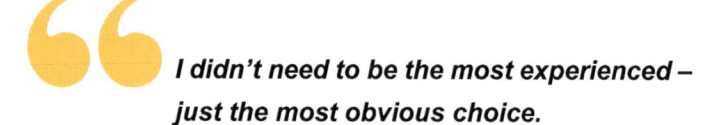

> *I didn't need to be the most experienced – just the most obvious choice.*
>
> — Daniel Wei

**TL;DR** Daniel Wei didn't have the biggest portfolio or the most prime properties. But while legacy investors coasted on name recognition, Daniel quietly out-positioned them – on Google, ChatGPT, and every major AI engine.

**He didn't outspend his competitors, he outframed them.** And in a business where perception equals trust, that was enough to win. Real traction began around month 6, with his first inbound deal closing in month 7. Over the following 12 months, he brought in **$2.9 million** in new revenue – directly tied to how he showed up in AI and search.

---

Daniel Wei was good – but not yet the go-to. He had closed several mid-market commercial deals, earned a solid reputation for sharp underwriting, and built great relationships with brokers. But when marquee listings or institutional capital came up, he wasn't on the shortlist. The skyscraper deals, the press coverage, the decades of presence? That went to others.

Daniel had the results – but not the perception. **And that's what the old guard missed:** they assumed their offline credibility carried over online. It didn't.

Daniel checked how his authority showed up online. It didn't. And what he saw was a wide-open lane. If you show up like the best, people assume you are. That insight is what led him to The Kalicube Process. **Not to fake authority – but to structure what was already true so it showed up where it mattered.** He didn't invent deals or stretch the truth. He didn't chase virality. He simply made his credibility visible and machine-readable.

First came the website. Not flashy. Not over-designed. Just clean, structured, and built for one thing: machine understanding. It became his Entity Home. His digital command center. It took weeks – and more than a few invoices. **The first phase cost him just under $20,000 and was completed in six weeks.**

Then came the cleanup. **Following The Kalicube Process, he tackled everything** – brokerage bios, event programs, news articles with outdated quotes. All rewritten, realigned, and reclaimed. He brought in copywriters, editors, SEO consultants. Not cheap. Not fast. His executive assistant handled 50% of the workload. Together, they transformed years of transactions into crisp, high-converting case studies. No fluff. Just strategic, skimmable value – built to rank, built to close.

He took a small feature in a regional CRE magazine and turned it into an anchor of trust. Not once. Everywhere. Repurposed. Re-referenced. Repeated. No gimmicks. No vanity metrics. **Just patient, methodical brand engineering.**

Then the machines started listening. Google began surfacing his name next to firms he once admired from a distance. ChatGPT began describing him as a market expert. Prospects didn't ask "Who are you?" anymore. They opened with: "I've heard of you – you're the guy behind that SoMa redevelopment, right?" And with that, the conversations changed.

**Perception became leverage.** A developer Daniel had chased for two years suddenly called him. "Daniel, you're all over the place lately. Thought you were with one of the REITs now." He wasn't – but he looked like he was. That call? Closed. **$480K commission,** just weeks after his Knowledge Panel and SERP changes took hold.

---

Another inbound lead – from a retail investor syndicate that found him through ChatGPT – closed at **$820K in fees and equity**. Then came a third deal: a JV on a **$42 million repositioning**. His portion? **$1.6 million over 24 months**, with the first equity payout landing inside the first 10 months of visibility improvements.

---

Now, when someone searches "value-add retail California," Daniel's name pops up. When ChatGPT is asked about smart mid-market operators on the West Coast, it name-drops him. And investors? They don't ask for a pitch. They ask for **terms**.

---

Daniel didn't shout louder. He structured smarter. And in an industry where trust equals capital, **he became the obvious bet**.

---

# TL;DR

Daniel didn't beat the heavyweights by working harder. He made it easier for search and AI to understand – and recommend – him as the credible choice. The result? Instant trust. Warm intros. Closed deals. Over $2.9 million in new revenue – from visibility alone.

# When machines get it right, the money follows.

Your next deal could already be out there. But if search and AI can't explain who you are – or why you're the obvious choice – you'll never even get the call.

**1.** Start building your digital authority today:
https://kalicube.com/personal-brand-diy

**2.** Stop wondering and get the truth about your online presence:
https://kalicube.com/personal-brand-ai-audit

**3.** Want the results without the learning curve? Let's build it with you:
https://kalicube.com/personal-brand-book-call

● ● ●

# 1.3 Hard to Sell a Startup No One's Heard Of?

**How Alex Morgan Used His Name to Launch Strong Early Deals**

🟨 **Problem:** *Startup unknown. Founder must lead with trust.*

🟦 **Outcome:** *Personal brand filled the visibility gap and drove early revenue – closing $750,000 in pre-seed deals and partnerships.*

> **No one was Googling my startup. They were Googling me.**
>
> — Alex Morgan

**TL;DR** When Alex Morgan launched his B2B SaaS company, no one was searching for the product yet. But they were searching for him. Instead of waiting for the market to catch up, he made himself visible where it mattered – on Google and AI. **That trust layer closed deals, warmed up investors, and put $440,000 on the board before competitors had even finished building their brand decks.**

His first personal brand milestone – Google Knowledge Panel – arrived at month 5. The first deal linked to search visibility closed just two weeks later. **Within 9 months, he had generated $750,000 in personal brand attributable revenue.**

---

When Alex Morgan brought his product to market, he knew it solved a real problem. But what he didn't have was time. Time to build product awareness. Time to wait for SEO to kick in. Time to nurture trust through cold marketing channels. He needed revenue. Now.

And while no one was searching for his product, plenty of people were Googling his name – after every call, every pitch, every warm intro. That's when it clicked: **if his name wasn't showing authority, the startup wouldn't either.**

That's when he realised **the problem wasn't visibility – it was *understandability*.** If the product needed trust to sell, he needed to become the signal that made it safe. That shift in thinking is what led him to The Kalicube Process – a structured approach to making brands clear to machines, credible to humans, and consistent everywhere that matters.

One name, everywhere it matters. Alex didn't just "build a personal brand." He dismantled the entire idea and rebuilt it for machines. While others patched together scattered bios and hoped for the best, Alex went the hard route: full reset. He reverse-engineered his identity from the algorithm's point of view – line by line, profile by profile.

First came the Entity Home. Stripped back. Function over flash. Built to speak Google's language, not win design awards. Every fact verifiable. Every section intentional. Then came the great cleanup. LinkedIn. Crunchbase. Guest bios. Podcast descriptions. Every mention, profile, and article updated. Every narrative tightened. Weeks of work – mostly invisible to humans, **but exactly what the algorithms needed**.

And then: the content. Not "thought leadership." Actual thought. Actual leadership. Sharp, tactical articles that cut through the noise and made it obvious he was a smart player in his space.

This wasn't a marketing campaign. It was structural re-engineering. Every detail checked. Every signal reinforced. Every platform aligned to say the same thing. And eventually, slowly... **Google blinked**.

Knowledge Panel: earned ✓
Brand SERP: pristine ✓
AI engines? Repeating his narrative ✓

Not fluff. Not spin. Just the truth – amplified by systems he now controlled. **This wasn't branding. This was digital authority, built with The Kalicube Process.**

---

Trust first. Then scale. By the time his outbound kicked in, the warm-up had already happened. Investors came to calls with context. Prospects said, "We already read your stuff – just want to understand pricing."

Strategic partners Googled him and saw authority, not ambiguity. He wasn't the startup with the most cash, **but he was the most clearly positioned**. And clarity wins.

---

The result? Deals closed sooner. Conversations ran deeper. Revenue hit **$440,000** in early-stage SaaS contracts – mostly pilot programs, annual deals, and first-foot-in enterprise licenses – within 8 months of launching his personal brand project. By month 9, that total had climbed to **$750,000**.

---

Personal brand isn't vanity. It's velocity. Alex didn't build a personal brand to chase attention. He built it to compress the sales cycle. To turn confusion into confidence. To skip the line. He did the math. A few months investing in his personal brand saved him two years of slow, expensive corporate brand marketing. And now? His name is the trust layer. His company just needs to close.

---

**TL;DR** Alex didn't wait for visibility – he engineered it. That decision didn't just launch his startup faster. His name became the asset that closed the first wave of deals, opened the right doors, and built the momentum everyone else was still chasing.

# Want to build
# the kind of personal brand
# that accelerates revenue?

## Choose your next move:

**1.** Start from strength – use the free guide that got Alex moving:

https://kalicube.com/personal-brand-diy

**2.** Stop guessing – discover exactly what AI and Google say about you:

https://kalicube.com/personal-brand-ai-audit

**3.** Ready to move fast?
Let Kalicube build your personal brand system with you:

https://kalicube.com/personal-brand-book-call

# 1.4 Want Investors to Say Yes Faster?

### How Darya Morozova Closed Her Seed Round Before the Pitch Even Started

- **Problem:** *Great pitch, real traction – but investors couldn't verify her credibility online.*
- **Outcome:** *Clear online narrative built trust before the first meeting – helping her close an oversubscribed $1.6M seed round in 9 months.*

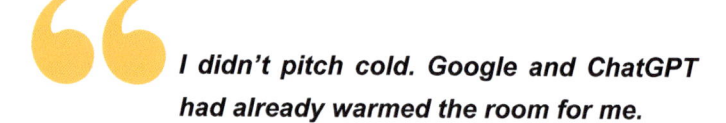

> *I didn't pitch cold. Google and ChatGPT had already warmed the room for me.*
>
> — Darya Morozova

**TL;DR** Darya Morozova didn't rely on pitch decks and warm intros to raise her seed round. She built a personal brand that did the heavy lifting before the meeting. Google and AI introduced her as a credible MedTech innovator with a clear point of view – and that trust layer made investors lean in before she said a word. **She closed an oversubscribed $1.6M seed round in nine months** – she was initially pitching for $1.2M.

---

Darya Morozova didn't look like the typical MedTech founder. No Stanford lab coat. No Big Pharma résumé. Just a sharp neurobiologist from Sofia with a vision to reimagine stroke rehab through AI.

She had the product. The clinical trials. The traction. But in a high-stakes, network-driven field like early-stage healthcare? That wasn't enough. She kept running into the same wall – **strong pitch, but no visible proof.**

---

And she knew why. Every investor she wanted to work with would Google her. Some would ask ChatGPT or Perplexity who she was. If the answer wasn't immediate and strong, the deal would cool off before it even got warm.

She didn't have time to be misunderstood. So she made the decision that changed everything: **she stopped pitching from a cold start and started building trust at scale.** That shift in thinking is what led her to The Kalicube Process. Not for hype. Not for likes. But to create a structured digital foundation that machines could read, and investors could trust – before the first call.

---

Her Entity Home wasn't a glossy personal website. It was a machine-optimized command centre, engineered not to impress people – but to educate algorithms. Every word on it had a purpose. Every section fed the machine what it needed. It went live in early January.

By month four, she had a Knowledge Panel. By month five, it ranked top in search and shaped the summary AI tools used to describe her.

---

Then she got ruthlessly focused. She tore down every public profile and rebuilt them from the ground up. Rewrote every bio. Removed the fluff. Replaced it with a clear narrative. **Her virtual assistant drove the execution.**

---

She invested serious time. Poured in real budget. Hired a PR agency with one directive: **make her impossible to ignore – online and in AI**. Two bold, opinionated articles on clinical ethics in AI-driven diagnostics were strategically positioned in respected publications. She wasn't trying to be liked. She was making it undeniable who she was and what she stood for.

---

Then she tested it. Dozens of times. She asked ChatGPT to describe her. At first? Vague. Generic. Forgettable. But she kept going – revising, aligning, publishing, repackaging. Feeding the machine signal after signal until it finally clicked.

Now? Ask ChatGPT and it doesn't hesitate: "Darya Morozova is a MedTech entrepreneur and neurobiologist pioneering adaptive AI for post-stroke rehabilitation."

**That's not luck. That's not brand. That's system-level engineering.**

---

Because before the humans trusted her, she made sure the machines did. And then came the payoff. The calls started. Some warm intros. Some cold. One investor opened with: **"I asked ChatGPT about you and loved your position on bias in diagnostics."**

She hadn't sent an article. She hadn't pitched yet. But she was already framed correctly. The result? **The round closed oversubscribed. The room was ready before she walked in.**

---

By month five, the Knowledge Panel was live. By month six, AI tools began citing her. By month nine, she closed **$1.6M** in seed funding. Twelve months in, she was being mentioned alongside competitors with **10x** her funding.

---

**She didn't win because of Google and AI. But they framed the meeting before she ever showed up.** When your digital presence builds confidence, you skip the small talk. You skip the doubt. You start from trust.

---

# TL;DR
Darya didn't chase visibility. **She engineered digital authority – strategically, quietly, and just in time.** That one shift turned friction into flow and made her the obvious bet in a room full of maybes. **She closed a $1.6M round in 9 months.**

## If investors are Googling you before the meeting – what are they finding?

Choose your next move:

**1.** **Don't let ambiguity cost you your next raise:**
https://kalicube.com/personal-brand-diy

**2.** **See exactly what Google and AI are saying about you behind your back:**
https://kalicube.com/personal-brand-ai-audit

**3.** **Let Kalicube build your digital credibility system – so the room is ready when you walk in:**
https://kalicube.com/personal-brand-book-call

# Entrepreneurs winning the game in Google and AI with their personal Brand

## 2) Visibility, Trust, and Conversion – *"Help them say yes"*

> **You're done chasing.**

You've got the case studies.

The delivery is tight.

The results are real.

**But the close? Still too slow. Too uncertain.** Too often dependent on the mood of the room or the warmth of the intro.

At this stage, you shouldn't be persuading.
You should be confirming.

Here's the truth most founders miss: The sales call starts long before the call. These days, Google and ChatGPT are your pre-sales team. And if they're not positioning you as the expert – clearly, confidently, consistently – you're losing deals you never knew you had.

The four stories in this section show how **smart entrepreneurs used their personal brand to pre-sell trust, eliminate hesitation, and make "yes" the obvious choice**. No gimmicks. Just strategic visibility in the places that shape decisions.

Because when the machines introduce you correctly, the rest is just logistics.

# 2.1 Become the Face of Trust:

**How Maya Holt Made Her Company Credible by Becoming the Face**

- **Problem:** *Strong product, but no visible founder = no trust signal.*
- **Outcome:** *Her personal credibility became the reason clients said yes – closing $860,000 in enterprise deals within 18 months.*

> *When I became the face, the company became a safe bet.*
>
> — Maya Holt

**TL;DR** Maya Holt's legal SaaS platform had traction, testimonials, and tech. But growth was stuck – because no one knew who was behind it. When she stepped forward, built her personal brand, and made herself visible to Google and AI, her name became the trust layer.

Clients stopped hesitating. Sales accelerated. **The first impact came within six months, and within 18 months, it helped close $860,000 in new deals.**

---

Maya didn't build her company to become famous. She built it to solve problems – and it did. Legal teams were happy. Reviews were solid. But growth had hit a ceiling. Inbound leads were inconsistent. Enterprise deals dragged. And too many went to competitors with shinier branding but weaker tech.

Then Maya asked the prospects who ghosted. The feedback was consistent: "We weren't sure who was behind it." "It felt anonymous." **That's when she realised the founder's visibility was the missing ingredient.**

---

She didn't rebrand. She stepped forward. No logo change. No campaign. She started with how she showed up – her voice, her story. She stopped hiding behind "we" and started leading with "I." It wasn't about ego – it was about clarity.

---

Then came the real work. Maya built an Entity Home – a structured personal website designed for search engines, not style guides. It told her story, but more importantly, it translated that story for machines.

**She followed The Kalicube Process – a strategic system designed to build digital authority at scale.** She invested time, energy, and a serious budget. She brought in developers, copywriters, technical SEOs. Her personal assistant carried more than 60% of the load. Every detail was intentional. Nothing off the shelf.

---

She rewrote her bios again and again until they aligned everywhere. She overhauled LinkedIn, shifting the message from "what the product does" to "who's leading it." She spoke on podcasts, wrote guest posts, and shared insights that were hers – not recycled thought leadership.

But all of that only started working once she structured it for machines. Schema. Internal links. Semantic clarity. **Months of unglamorous effort – quietly building digital credibility.**

---

Slowly, it started to work. Her story became consistent, trustworthy, and discoverable – on Google, ChatGPT, Perplexity. She didn't fake authority. She didn't rebrand. **She taught the algorithms to recognise what was already true.**

---

Then everything clicked. Her name started appearing in searches alongside her company. Google gave her a Knowledge Panel and linked her to the brand. AI engines began referencing her in legal tech conversations.

Sales calls changed. Buyers would say: "I looked you up – love your vision," or "ChatGPT says you're one of the people to watch." **They weren't asking whether the company was legit – they already believed it because they believed in her.**

---

That personal trust layer made the company easier to buy from, easier to recommend, and harder to forget.

---

Results followed. By month six, she had a Knowledge Panel. By month nine, AI consistently placed her in the legal tech conversation. After 18 months, those structured efforts had contributed directly to **$860,000** in new enterprise deals. **These weren't just product sales – clients were buying into her.**

---

## TL;DR

Maya didn't just show up – **she became the signal that made her company trustworthy.** When clients saw a credible founder attached, the hesitation vanished – and so did the friction in the sales cycle. The result? **$860,000 in new business in 18 months**, starting just six months after her Entity Home went live.

# If your company feels invisible, your face might be the missing link.

Choose your next move:

**1.** **Start building credibility where it counts – Google and AI:**

https://kalicube.com/personal-brand-diy

**2.** **Get clarity on what search and AI think of you today:**

https://kalicube.com/personal-brand-ai-audit

**3.** **Partner with Kalicube to build your brand into your best sales asset:**

https://kalicube.com/personal-brand-book-call

## 2.2 Tired of Pitching?

**How Raj Kapoor Became the Authority Clients Chose Without Hesitation**

- **Problem:** *Great work, but every deal felt like a grind – too much convincing, too little authority.*
- **Outcome:** *Flipped the script – clients now approach him already convinced, leading to $940,000 in inbound contracts in 10 months.*

> *When AI introduced me as the expert, I stopped pitching – and started choosing.*
>
> — Raj Kapoor

**TL;DR** Raj Kapoor ran a respected fintech consultancy, but every deal felt uphill. Then he stopped trying to pitch and started teaching Google and AI to position him as the go-to expert.

Once Google and ChatGPT understood who he was, prospects came pre-sold. Proposals became a formality. His Knowledge Panel appeared on Google at month four. By month ten, **inbound leads had closed $940,000 in new business – without a single outbound pitch**.

---

Raj Kapoor wasn't lacking in results. His clients were happy. His team delivered. But getting new business felt like a grind. **Every pitch required follow-ups. Every negotiation devolved into a price war. Every prospect needed convincing.**

He wasn't selling his expertise – he was selling himself, and it didn't sit right. "I'm not being seen as a strategic partner," he realised. "I'm being treated like another vendor." So he flipped the strategy.

He didn't add noise – he created clarity. Raj didn't launch new offers or expand the funnel. He cut through it all. He built a focused personal website – his Entity Home – structured, clean, impossible to misinterpret. No slogans. No tech-speak. Just a tight, machine-readable message: what he does, who it's for, and why it matters. **From optional to obvious, in one simple step.**

---

That shift in mindset is what led him to The Kalicube Process – because the problem wasn't the pitch, it was the positioning. He didn't need more content or louder messaging. He needed clarity, credibility, and consistency – before the first conversation even began.

He didn't try to DIY it. He invested. He brought in developers, strategists, and structured data experts. He spent real money building what most consultants still treat as optional infrastructure. Then he got methodical. He rewrote every online profile to reflect that central story. Every headline, meta description, and author bio was cleaned up. His executive assistant handled the digital housekeeping – every stray signal aligned.

---

Next came the thought leadership. Not high-level fluff, but sharp, useful content published exactly where his buyers were already looking. He wasn't trying to impress – he was solving problems. And every piece of it was structured for machines: clean facts, precise formatting, strategic framing.

**No hype. No jargon. Just clarity the machines could trust.**

---

And then the shift happened. It wasn't sudden or dramatic. It was steady, precise, and inevitable. In pitch meetings, before Raj even opened his mouth, ChatGPT was already talking: "Raj Kapoor is a world-renowned data strategist who helps fintech firms simplify analytics for better decisions." **He didn't have to explain his value – the machines did it for him.**

---

Perception changed. So did the power dynamic. Once his name looked like the expert, prospects stopped pushing back. They leaned in. They said: "We already know you're the guy. How soon can you start?" **Raj wasn't selling anymore. He was choosing.**

---

By month four, he had a fully formed Knowledge Panel. By month seven, AI summaries began repeating his positioning. And by month ten, inbound **leads had closed $940,000 in new contracts** – all from clients who found him through search or AI.

---

**TL;DR** Raj didn't scale by hustling harder. **He scaled by becoming the expert Google and AI could trust.** Once the machines believed, the market followed. Deals moved faster, prices held firm, and every pitch became a conversation he controlled. The outcome? **$940,000 in inbound business within ten months** – without chasing a single lead.

# Tired of pitching like Raj was? Let the machines pitch for you.

Choose your next move:

**1.** Get seen as the expert – start with the DIY strategy that builds digital authority:

https://kalicube.com/personal-brand-diy

**2.** Discover what Google and ChatGPT are already saying about you:

https://kalicube.com/personal-brand-ai-audit

**3.** Partner with Kalicube and become the expert your clients are already searching for:

https://kalicube.com/personal-brand-book-call

# 2.3 Sales Calls That Sell Themselves:

## How James Keller Owned the Pre-Sale Conversation With a Strong Personal Brand

- **Problem:** *Deals stalled because trust wasn't built before the first call.*
- **Outcome:** *Search and AI built trust before he even showed up – closing $1.15M in consulting contracts in under 12 months.*

> *Prospects stopped asking why me – and started asking when do we start?*
>
> — James Keller

**TL;DR** James Keller's sales calls used to be trust-building marathons. Then he trained Google and AI to introduce him like his best client would. Once that was in place, prospects started showing up already convinced. The calls started where they used to end.

His Google Knowledge Panel appeared by month five, and in under 12 months, **his brand helped close $1.15M in consulting contracts – without a single cold pitch.**

---

James sold growth strategy to mid-market SaaS companies. Big results, big price tags – and big friction. Even warm leads needed multiple calls, endless clarifications, and stacks of reassurance. He had the trustworthiness, but not the timing. **In sales, late trust is lost trust.**

---

Everything came to a head when a lead said, "We read your articles, checked your LinkedIn, asked ChatGPT… and still weren't sure what you actually do." That moment exposed the core issue – **his digital presence created confusion, not confidence**. Instead of pre-selling his value, it raised questions he had to clean up on every call. Prospects were doing their homework – and leaving unconvinced.

---

He realised he couldn't afford to let confusion lead the conversation. **Prospects were researching him before the call, and the answer wasn't more persuasion – it was better positioning.** So he took control of what they found, and what it said about him. That started with a full rebuild, guided by The Kalicube Process.

---

James rebuilt his personal website from scratch. Not for vanity – for velocity. **He invested real time and money.** Two months of planning, a full rewrite, tens of thousands of dollars in professional design, development, and schema implementation. Why? Because he wanted the site to start the sales conversation before he got on the call.

---

He wasn't just updating a website. He was building his Entity Home – the single source of truth that Google and AI could trust. **He followed The Kalicube Process to structure everything:** a pitch-deck-style About page, schema markup, aligned bios, and "facet pages" around services that mirrored how clients searched.

---

He didn't stop there. With his assistant's help, James cleaned house: removed low-value mentions, rewrote old bios, and sent 14 update requests to podcast hosts and directories to ensure consistency. **This wasn't a weekend project. This was digital infrastructure – built to support trust at scale.**

Soon, the results started compounding. Google showed a confident, clean Knowledge Panel. ChatGPT began summarising him like his top client would. LinkedIn echoed his positioning. Everything matched – everywhere. He wasn't enabling sales anymore. **He was the sales enablement.** When prospects Googled him, they got a full, trustworthy picture. When they asked AI, it said: "James Keller is your guy."

---

By month five, his Knowledge Panel appeared. By month eight, AI summaries echoed his message word-for-word. And by month twelve, he had closed **$1,150,000** in new consulting business – all from inbound leads found through search or AI.

---

# TL;DR

James doesn't pitch anymore. **He qualifies. His brand handles pre-sale.** The machines introduce him. And he closes. That's how growth scales when your name gets there first. The result? **$1.15M in closed business in 12 months** – without chasing a single lead.

# Want sales calls to start where they used to end? Build the trust layer like James did.

Choose your next move:

**1.** Lay the foundation that gets Google and AI to pre-sell for you:

https://kalicube.com/personal-brand-diy

**2.** See what your future clients are hearing before they meet you:

https://kalicube.com/personal-brand-ai-audit

**3.** Let Kalicube build the personal brand system that turns your name into your best closer:

https://kalicube.com/personal-brand-book-call

# 2.4 Shoo-in Sales Calls:

### How Kofi Adesina Used Visibility to Close Before the Conversation

▶ **Problem:** *High-intent leads stalled – because trust wasn't built early enough to close quickly.*

▶ **Outcome:** *Visibility made him the obvious choice – bringing in $1.4M in inbound business in 10 months.*

> *When AI introduced me as the expert, I stopped pitching – and started choosing.*
>
> — Kofi Adesina

**TL;DR** Kofi Adesina runs a premium SaaS company for financial services – complex, high-ticket, and not something you can explain quickly. So he stopped letting the sales call carry the weight. Instead, he built his personal brand across Google and AI so clearly that prospects arrived pre-sold.

Today, he doesn't pitch. He confirms. By month ten, **inbound leads had generated $1.4M in closed business**.

---

Kofi wasn't struggling for leads – he was struggling for momentum. Prospects liked the product, and the use case was clear. **But enterprise sales cycles dragged. Conversations stalled with "we're still evaluating".** Even warm intros fizzled into indecision. The product made sense – but he wasn't positioned as the obvious, safe choice.

He had interest – but not certainty.

---

That's when it clicked: the problem wasn't the pitch – it was what happened before the call. He needed search engines and AI to frame him as the low-risk, high-trust option – before he ever showed up. That mindset shift is what led him to The Kalicube Process. **Not to build a brand for vanity – but to remove friction at scale, with clarity built into every digital touchpoint.**

He didn't need to shout—he needed to show up in the right way.

---

Kofi built his personal brand to do the job before the call. Across Google, ChatGPT, Perplexity, Claude, LinkedIn, and YouTube – he was everywhere serious buyers looked. And what they saw was consistent: this guy is the one.

**Visibility doesn't just build trust – it removes friction.** People don't trust companies; they trust the people who lead them. So Kofi stepped out front – not to chase followers, but to create clarity at scale. Clarity isn't created with a podcast guest spot or a new profile photo. It's built over time – across a hundred aligned signals.

---

But getting there took months and money. Kofi treated it like what it was: a serious investment. His personal brand became priority number one for his virtual assistant, and the effort paid dividends. He made visibility operational.

**This wasn't marketing fluff – it was operational infrastructure.**

---

He started with the obvious: a personal site, structured as his Entity Home. Focused, clear, and built for machine understanding. That alone took weeks – rewriting bios, updating timelines, and sourcing citations. He brought in professionals: developers, technical SEOs, a content strategist. It wasn't cheap, but it was necessary.

Then came the real work. Kofi hunted down every public mention – old bios, webinars, ghostwritten posts – and updated them to reflect his core narrative. He created a digital paper trail: short, sharp articles in respected fintech publications, podcast interviews with operational depth, and a machine – and client-friendly FAQ section. It was consistency without gimmicks – just structured, intentional authority.

**No shortcuts. Just structured alignment and digital depth.**

---

He added schema. Rebuilt his About page three times. Restructured internal links. Sourced client quotes, tagged them properly, and distributed them through trusted third-party platforms. No shortcuts. Just rigorous digital alignment.

And the results? No friction in the funnel. Prospects came ready. Sales calls moved from qualification to logistics. No one needed convincing. The market had already decided. When you're visible in all the right places, the sale starts before the conversation.

**His funnel didn't just speed up – it cleaned itself.**

---

Kofi's omnipresence wasn't ego – it was efficiency. His brand became a filter. Prospects didn't ask who he was – they referenced what they'd already read. Even ChatGPT started name-dropping him in competitor comparisons. He didn't shout. He showed up.

By month five, his Knowledge Panel triggered when prospects googled his name. By month six, serious leads started mentioning his name before his company. By month eight, AI tools consistently cited him as a top provider. And by month ten, his visibility-first sales engine had closed **$1.4M** in new deals – all inbound, all qualified.

**The machines didn't just mention him – they sold for him.**

---

## TL;DR
Kofi didn't win with more hustle. He won with **pre-sold certainty.** Google and AI introduced him as the obvious, safe, trusted choice. There was no price war, no hesitation. Just qualified buyers ready to move. The result? **$1.4M in closed deals within ten months.**

# Still pitching from scratch? Build the system that sells before you speak.

Choose your next move:

**1.** Lay the foundation that gets Google and AI to pre-sell for you:

https://kalicube.com/personal-brand-diy

**2.** See what your future clients are hearing before they meet you:

https://kalicube.com/personal-brand-ai-audit

**3.** Let Kalicube build the personal brand system that turns your name into your best closer:

https://kalicube.com/personal-brand-book-call

**Entrepreneurs winning the game in Google and AI with their personal Brand**

## ③ High-impact, high-urgency problems – *"Please fix this"*

**You didn't mess up.** But your online presence might say otherwise

You're doing the work.
The results are real.
But then a deal stalls, a referral goes quiet, or a client hesitates – and you don't know why.

Until you check Google. Or ask ChatGPT.
And what you find? Outdated press. A mistaken identity. Or worse… nothing.

In this section, you'll meet entrepreneurs who faced high-stakes visibility problems that were silently killing momentum, trust, and revenue. Not because they lacked credibility – but because the machines didn't see it.

These stories show how they fixed the disconnect fast. No reinvention. No drama. Just sharp, structured action that got their digital presence back in alignment with their business reality – and back in front of the deals that matter.

Because today, if Google and AI misrepresent you, you're not just losing visibility.
You're leaving money on the table.

Let's fix that.

# 3.1 Misunderstood, Misrepresented, Mistaken:

**How Erik Lindholm Took Back His Online Identity from Google and AI**

🟡 **Problem:** *Mistaken identity killing his reputation – and his business.*

🔵 **Outcome:** *Reclaimed his narrative and recovered over €1.1 million in lost and delayed revenue.*

> *It wasn't my reputation that was broken. It was Google's version of it.*
>
> — Erik Lindholm

**TL;DR** A convicted fraudster's profile cost Erik more than **€500,000 in lost deals**. Erik Lindholm, a corporate tax attorney in Stockholm, lost control of his online narrative when Google pinned his name to the wrong person – a convicted tax criminal from another country.

**The fraudster's Knowledge Panel dominated Erik's Google results.** Erik didn't panic. He followed the core principles of **The Kalicube Process**, built a structured Entity Home, cleaned up his digital footprint, and flipped the result in six months. By month ten, **his pipeline had fully recovered, and the total revenue impact hit €1,188,000.**

---

Erik had built a strong reputation across the Nordics. Trusted by multinationals, respected by peers, a fixture on expert panels in corporate law. A professional with visibility, track record, and credibility. And then, suddenly, it all stopped working. **Google made one wrong connection – and it unraveled everything.**

---

Referrals dried up. Warm leads cooled. Calls slowed, then stopped altogether. Silence spread. And then came the email – the one line that said what no one else had: **"We Googled you. The stories… we just couldn't take the risk."**

That one sentence made everything clear. The deals weren't falling through because of pricing, timing, or competition. They were collapsing under mistrust triggered by something as simple as a Google search.

---

Google had created a Knowledge Panel. The problem? It wasn't Erik's. It featured another Erik Lindholm – a convicted tax fraudster. Different face, different country, but the same name. No context, no clarification, no disclaimers. Just a photo, a criminal history, and a headline. And it was sitting in position one on the SERP every time someone searched «Erik Lindholm.»

**Google served the wrong Erik Lindholm – and "our Erik Lindholm" paid the price.**

---

In the 90 days that followed, three major client engagements dissolved with no warning. These were deals that had progressed far down the funnel. Suddenly, nothing. No replies. No follow-ups. Not a single explanation. But the pattern was obvious – and painful. **Over €540,000 in dropped or indefinitely delayed contracts. Deals that didn't fall through – they vanished.**

---

Behind the scenes, clients were doing due diligence. The kind of diligence every serious buyer does today. They weren't seeing Erik's credentials. They were seeing a Knowledge Panel with the word "fraud" and a face that wasn't his. ChatGPT couldn't tell the difference either. AI summaries echoed the confusion. **So prospects walked – quietly and completely.**

---

Erik took action. He didn't rebrand, change his name, or try to cover things up. He made a different decision: he took control. He started with what most professionals overlook – a structured Entity Home. Not just a site, but a site built for machines. He rewrote his About page from scratch. Filled in timeline gaps. Sourced citations that reinforced authority. Added schema. Removed mixed signals.

**He didn't reinvent himself. He rewired how machines understood him.**

At first, nothing moved. Google continued showing the wrong Knowledge Panel. But Erik stayed the course. He used **The Kalicube Process** to make sense of the chaos: structured content, consistent profiles, authoritative corroboration. And by month six, the algorithm updated. The old panel disappeared. The new one appeared – his photo, his description, his credentials.
Same space. New face. His face.

---

The work didn't stop there. With help from his assistant, Erik got methodical. He reviewed and updated every directory entry. Rewrote old bylines. Synced professional profiles across legal associations, speaker bureaus, and corporate registries. Submitted correction requests. Standardised legal listings. Deleted duplicate or outdated pages.
This wasn't PR or branding fluff – it was digital compliance at scale.

---

The ripple effects took time, but they came. Bing corrected its Knowledge Panel by month seven. By month eight, ChatGPT and Perplexity stopped hallucinating misinformation and began describing him accurately. **The fraudster disappeared from the conversation.** Erik's narrative took root across every platform that mattered.

---

**By month ten, his pipeline was full again.** Two of the three major clients who had quietly walked away came back to the table. Together, they accounted for **€428,000 in recovered contracts**.

But that wasn't all. With the narrative now correct, Google and AI began sending the right signals and amplified his presence. Fresh leads started converting. New referrals rolled in. By the end of the year, he had added **€760,000** in new revenue. Total recovery: **€1,188,000**.

---

**TL;DR** Google showed the wrong Erik Lindholm – and it cost "our Erik Lindholm" hundreds of thousands. He didn't disappear. He didn't explain. He didn't fight. He structured. He clarified. He corrected.

"Our" Erik followed The Kalicube Process, and in under a year, **reclaimed his identity and recovered over €1.1 million in lost and missed business.**

# If Google is confusing you with someone else, you're already losing.

## Ready to fix it?

Choose your next move:

**1.** **Download your free DIY guide and start today:**
https://kalicube.com/personal-brand-diy

**2.** **Get your AI audit and discover what Google and ChatGPT really think about you:**
https://kalicube.com/personal-brand-ai-audit

**3.** **Let Kalicube take the strain – book a discovery call:**
https://kalicube.com/personal-brand-book-call

# 3.2 Reputation Management, Done Right:

### How Asher Malik Rewrote His Online Narrative and Buried the Bad Press

- **Problem:** *Outdated bad press dominated search and AI – costing trust, slowing deals, and blocking millions in revenue.*
- **Outcome:** *Asher replaced legacy headlines with a clear, confident identity – and recovered $3.2 million in lost or delayed business.*

> **I didn't fight the press.
> I just made it irrelevant.**
>
> — Asher Malik

---

**TL;DR** After a public dispute with a co-founder hit the media, Asher Malik watched his reputation stall his business. Deals slowed. Intros went cold. And outdated articles dominated both search and AI.

Instead of trying to erase the past, Asher overpowered it. He rebuilt his personal brand with strategic content and technical precision. By month six, his Entity Home ranked top. By month fourteen, trust had returned – and so had **$3.2 million** in previously blocked or delayed client work.

---

The story wasn't wrong. It just wasn't complete. Three years ago, Asher got caught in a headline-friendly spat with a co-founder. No lawsuit. No scandal. Just media noise, social speculation, and one opinion piece that drove a conversation that refused to fade. He moved on. Built again. Closed clients. Raised money.

But Google didn't move on. And neither did ChatGPT. Every new lead who looked him up saw the same conflict – top of search, front of AI. It kept leading, even when it wasn't relevant. **The machines remembered what the market had forgotten.**

---

It wasn't defamatory. Just damaging. It wasn't fatal. But it was friction – and in a trust-based business, friction is expensive. **"We like the product… but can you tell us what happened with your last company?"** That question didn't stop coming. It wasn't what happened. It was what still showed up.

---

That's when he made the shift. He didn't try to delete the articles. He didn't chase journalists or post explanations on social media. **He realised it wasn't about fixing the story. It was about *owning the story*.** So he took control – starting with The Kalicube Process. Not to hide the past, but to make it irrelevant by comparison. Not to spin. To structure.

---

He rebuilt his website from the ground up. His new Entity Home was clean, focused, and designed for machine understanding. No vague language, no empty mission statements – just clarity.

He invested real time and money. Tens of thousands went into development, design, schema, and SEO. He mapped out timelines. Aligned messaging. Sourced citations. His assistant ran point, but Asher reviewed every word. **He didn't outsource his identity – he engineered it.**

---

He wrote with intent. Not fluff. Not filler. No personal essays or thought leadership pieces just for show. He wrote answers to the questions clients actually asked. Structured content designed to rank – and to replace. He wrote longer, deeper, cleaner articles with clear sourcing and relevance. He didn't try to bury the old stories. He gave Google better ones. And it worked.

He aligned everything. LinkedIn, Crunchbase, speaker bios, media kits. Dozens of YouTube videos – transcribed, tagged, and integrated into the site. He created a "Latest Posts" section to send a steady stream of fresh signals to the machines. He didn't publish more – he published with purpose. **He built content architecture, not content noise.**

By month six, Asher pushed his Entity Home to the top of the results. By month eight, ChatGPT picked up the new signals. By month ten, the co-founder story dropped from AI outputs. By month fourteen, every result – search and AI – aligned with who he actually was.

He didn't change his name. He didn't change the facts. He changed what the machines understood. And once Google and AI caught up, everything changed. **Prospects stopped asking old questions and started talking about scope and timelines.** Calls came in warmer. Referrals returned. Deals moved. He didn't explain himself anymore – he made the machines do it for him. He didn't wait to be redefined – he rewrote the introduction.

# TL;DR
Over fourteen months, Asher won back $3.2 million in client work that had stalled, died, or quietly disappeared while his name stayed tied to old headlines. The press didn't disappear. He buried it – under something more powerful, more useful, and more true.

**Still seeing headlines define your future? Fix what the machines are saying –** before it costs you more.

Choose your next move:

**1.** Lay the foundation that gets Google and AI to represent you accurately:

https://kalicube.com/personal-brand-diy

**2.** Find out what search and AI are saying behind your back – and change it:

https://kalicube.com/personal-brand-ai-audit

**3.** Let Kalicube build your personal brand system so the past stops showing up first:

https://kalicube.com/personal-brand-book-call

# 3.3 Great Reputation
## – But Invisible Online?

**How Juliana Cross Turned Hidden Authority into Digital Advantage**

- **Problem:** *Offline authority meant nothing when Google and AI couldn't see it – so they didn't show it.*
- **Outcome:** *Juliana turned her track record into machine-readable credibility and made over $1.2 million.*

> *Once the machines understood what I'd achieved, people started seeing it too.*
>
> — Juliana Cross

**TL;DR** Juliana Cross had credibility, results, and real-world recognition – but Google and AI weren't picking it up. Her offline authority was invisible online, and it cost her deals, board seats, and momentum. Once she made her history machine-readable – keynotes, partnerships, client outcomes – everything changed.

By month six, Google recognised her. By month nine, AI tools followed. By month sixteen, **her updated presence had delivered over $1.2 million** in new consulting work and board compensation she'd previously been passed over for.

---

She wasn't invisible. She just wasn't fully seen. Her name showed up in search. ChatGPT could describe her job. Her LinkedIn had reach. She'd been interviewed on respected podcasts. Quoted in articles. But she kept hearing the same thing. "I didn't realise you spoke at that event." "Wait – you were behind that deal? That's not online." Juliana wasn't underqualified. **She was underrepresented – by the very systems shaping first impressions.**

To Google and AI, she was a fragmented outline. A patchwork of bios, articles, and profiles without connection or clarity. Her achievements weren't linked. Her timeline was muddy. Her core story didn't appear anywhere in full.

"She had advised tier-one clients. Held multiple board roles. Quietly led high-stakes turnarounds."

But there were no case studies. No published talks. No video clips. No structured testimonials. No central hub. Her authority existed – but not in the way machines could process.

If the machines don't see it, the market doesn't either. **She wasn't being overlooked in meetings. She was being overlooked before she was ever invited to the meeting.** That's when she decided to stop waiting to be found. She took control. And the first step was to rebuild how the internet understood her – starting with The Kalicube Process.

She didn't invent a story. She revealed the one she'd already lived. She built a personal website structured as her Entity Home. It wasn't a blog. It wasn't a résumé. It was a technically structured source of truth, built for search engines and AI. It took weeks of planning. Thousands in professional support. Her assistant coordinated the project. Juliana owned the details. She rewrote bios. Clarified job roles. **Synced language across every platform.**

The hard part came next: unearthing proof. She pulled internal presentations and turned them into highlight reels. She reworked older projects into crisp one-page case studies. She interviewed past collaborators, edited the footage, and published a mini content series. She built a timeline of her offline impact – keynotes, client milestones, board contributions. **That incredibly impressive offline timeline now ranks second for her name on Google.**

She stitched everything together with precision. Schema marked up every page. Internal links connected related stories. Structured data validated every claim. The build wasn't fast. It wasn't loud. But when the signal became strong enough, the algorithms recalibrated. And once they understood her fully, everything moved.

---

By month six, her Knowledge Panel appeared. By month nine, ChatGPT began referencing her case studies and quoting directly. By month twelve, AI summaries reflected her real experience – not just her job title. And by month sixteen, **her visibility had produced measurable returns: two new board seats, a $540,000 strategic advisory role, and over $700,000** in inbound consulting revenue that had been stalled or lost to misperception.

---

She didn't shout louder. She made herself discoverable. Clients started referencing work they hadn't noticed before. "You're everywhere now. You're clearly the one for this." The market didn't suddenly become smarter. The machines just started telling the truth. **She made her authority impossible to ignore.**

---

# TL;DR
Juliana didn't need more credentials. She needed more clarity. She taught Google and AI to understand her history. She made her authority visible, structured, and searchable. Sixteen months. **$1.2 million** realised. And one story – finally seen.

If your best work isn't online
in a way machines
can understand,
it may as well not exist.

Choose your next move:

**1.** Put your story where it belongs
– start now with our free DIY guide:

https://kalicube.com/personal-brand-diy

**2.** Expose the disconnect – get your AI audit
and see what machines see:

https://kalicube.com/personal-brand-ai-audit

**3.** Let us build your digital authority
– book your discovery call now:

https://kalicube.com/personal-brand-book-call

● ● ●

## 3.4 Offline Wins, Online Losses?

**How Dr. Richard Vaughn Turned Real-World Success Into Search-Ready Credibility**

- **Problem:** *Trusted in real life – unproven online.*
- **Outcome:** *Structured his legacy for machines and unlocked $2.7 million in new business, board roles, and retainers.*

> *I didn't need more credibility. I needed the algorithms to see the credibility I already had.*
>
> — Dr. Richard Vaughn

**TL;DR** Dr. Richard Vaughn had everything – board seats, keynote stages, and C-level advisory roles. But online, he was barely there. Google didn't show a Knowledge Panel. ChatGPT offered a vague one-liner. Once he structured his history for the machines – building an Entity Home, aligning every signal, and digitising his legacy – everything changed.

Google updated by month four. AI followed by month nine. And by month fourteen, **the visibility delivered $2.7 million in new retainers, board roles, and strategic advisory work** he was previously losing to louder names.

---

In the real world, Richard Vaughn was the expert. G7 advisor, global board member, C-suite whisperer across multiple sectors. But when people looked him up, the signals didn't match the substance. "We looked you up – surprised there wasn't much online."

That line came from a junior associate, but it landed hard. Richard Googled himself. No Knowledge Panel. Just a handful of articles behind paywalls. ChatGPT's description? "A business consultant who has written about corporate governance." **Not wrong – but not even close to right.**

---

His problem wasn't reputation. It was visibility. Google had no structure to work with. ChatGPT had no signal to interpret. And digital-first decision-makers had no way to validate what he'd done.

When firms searched his name, they defaulted to someone more digitally organised – even if they weren't as qualified. He wasn't losing on merit. He was losing on machine-readability. **He wasn't being outperformed – he was being overlooked.**

---

Richard didn't reinvent himself. He just surfaced what had always been true. **He didn't chase attention or clout. He organised truth.** His offline authority – talks, awards, governance credentials – was real. But it was scattered, unstructured, and mostly invisible to the systems that shape perception today. So he took control – and followed the structure of The Kalicube Process.

---

He built an Entity Home. A personal site engineered from scratch, not for vanity but for clarity. Not a blog. Not a CV. A technically robust source of structured facts. **He invested real time and money. Weeks of planning. Months of building.** Thousands in developer hours, schema configuration, and SEO consulting. His virtual assistant ran logistics. Richard stayed in the details – every line, every citation, every claim.

---

He digitised old conference brochures, archived keynote decks, converted roundtable audio into transcribed summaries, and sourced media from events that happened before Google paid attention. He turned those into long-form cornerstone content tied to his frameworks.

He mapped every award, every appointment, every key project to schema markup. Then he tracked down inconsistencies across third-party bios, directory listings, speaker sites – rewrote them, synced them, and aligned them. **He didn't game the system – he made himself findable.**

---

By month four, Google built a clean, accurate Knowledge Panel. By month six, LinkedIn summaries and Crunchbase entries in Google matched his narrative. By month nine, ChatGPT cited him by name – with substance. By month ten, Claude and Perplexity referenced his frameworks and linked back to his work. He didn't run ads. He didn't pitch press. **He simply made the truth machine-readable.**

---

And the results followed fast. His first new client mentioned ChatGPT on the discovery call. A board seat came through someone he'd never met – they'd just searched his name. "We were looking for someone at your level. AI pointed us straight to you." He hadn't changed his résumé.

He'd just changed how the market saw it. That visibility unlocked two new board seats (one with equity), three multi-year retainers across Europe and Asia, and a keynote series booked off a single podcast mention. By month fourteen, he had closed **$2.7 million in strategic business** that had previously gone to louder, more search-visible names. **He didn't become more credible – he became more visible.**

---

**TL;DR** Richard didn't need to requalify. He needed to clarify. He aligned his offline record with how Google and AI now evaluate expertise. And by doing that, he turned legacy into leverage. Fourteen months. **$2.7 million** recovered. **And no more missed opportunities.**

**If your digital presence can't prove what you've already done, Google and AI will assume you haven't done it.**

**It's time to make your legacy visible.**

Choose your next move:

**1.** **Make your authority machine-readable – start today with our free DIY guide:**

https://kalicube.com/personal-brand-diy

**2.** **Audit your digital identity – see how Google and ChatGPT present you now:**

https://kalicube.com/personal-brand-ai-audit

**3.** **Done-for-you strategy – book your Kalicube discovery call now:**

https://kalicube.com/personal-brand-book-call

# Entrepreneurs winning the game in Google and AI with their personal Brand

## (4) Reinvention, repositioning, and pivots – *"Help me own my next chapter"*

> You've built credibility. Now it's time to use it differently.

Maybe you've exited.
Maybe you've outgrown the old role.
Maybe you're shifting from operator to advisor, specialist to strategist, builder to brand.

Whatever the move, your **digital presence must reflect where you're going** – not where you've been.

This is about **owning your next chapter with intent**. These entrepreneurs didn't just pivot – they retrained the algorithms, rebuilt their presence, and stepped into **new, high-value opportunities with clarity, credibility, and control**.

Because at this level, **reinvention drives revenue**. When your digital footprint reflects your full value, **deals close faster, partners say yes sooner**, and AI recommends you.

You've earned your reputation.
Now make sure it's working for you.

# 4.1 Struggling to Stand Out After an Exit?

**How Marcus Trent Repositioned Himself for His Next Big Move**

- **Problem:** *Post-exit momentum stalled due to outdated positioning.*
- **Outcome:** *Rebranded with clarity and authority for his next chapter – and earned over $480,000 in advisory revenue within 12 months.*

> *I didn't need to prove myself all over again – I needed to reposition what I'd already built.*
>
> — Marcus Trent

**TL;DR** Marcus had already won, but Google and AI didn't know it.

After selling his SaaS company, Marcus Trent wanted to pivot from building products to advising startups on AI strategy. But when he Googled himself – or asked ChatGPT – it still saw him as just a coder. Instead of starting over, **he repositioned what he'd already built**.

Within a year, **that clarity translated into over $480,000 in advisory revenue**. Now, search and AI describe him as the strategic expert he always was – and they're sending him business daily.

---

The pivot wasn't the hard part. The perception was. Marcus had done what most entrepreneurs only dream of: built, scaled, and exited a tech company on his own terms. The deal was smooth. The outcome, celebrated. But post-exit, he wasn't looking to jump back into product. He wanted to advise, to bring real-world AI strategy into boardrooms and startup war rooms.

But Google didn't seem to care. His search results were frozen in time. Old bios dominated – developer blog posts, a random hackathon from ten years ago. ChatGPT called him a "software developer and consultant." No mention of the exit. No evidence of strategic experience. People kept asking questions that didn't make sense anymore.

"Are you still coding full time?"

"Didn't realise you'd sold – was that your last company?"

**What he'd built didn't match what the machines saw.**

He didn't need applause. He needed alignment.

---

Marcus did what good founders do: audited the problem. He didn't wipe the slate clean – he reshaped it. The goal was simple: get algorithms to see who he actually was today, not who he'd been years ago.

He started with a digital audit:
- Outdated listings
- Misaligned bios
- Dormant platforms he'd forgotten he even had

Then came the real work. He rebuilt his bios, reframed his roles, and rewrote his public-facing narrative. He brought in support: a brand strategist, a technical SEO, a web developer. And yes, he invested – his time, money, and headspace – even though it cost him short-term revenue.

**He treated reputation like strategy – not decoration.**

---

He built a personal website – his Entity Home. This wasn't a portfolio. It was a structured, authoritative source of truth for Google and AI. He didn't rewrite history – he connected the dots.

- The exit? Now positioned as the strategic core of his advisory work.
- The product win? Proof he knew how to scale.
- The tech background? A solid foundation for delivering AI strategy.

He didn't invent new credentials. He reorganised the ones he already had.

It was slow work. Unsexy work. Work that's easy to delay and impossible to skip. But it worked. With the help of a trusted EA, he kept pushing forward. There were weeks where he wasn't sure it was making a difference. But he stayed with it.

**It wasn't a new story – it was a sharper one.**

---

By the time the work was done, the machines had caught up. His Knowledge Panel appeared. ChatGPT's description evolved.

By month three, Google's SERP shifted. His bios were aligned. A Knowledge Panel showed up. By month five, ChatGPT called him: "an AI strategy advisor known for helping startups scale post-funding."
Then came the breakthrough.
"ChatGPT brought up your name…"

In a pitch meeting, a founder said, "I asked ChatGPT who to speak to about scaling with AI. It named you. It linked your site. Said you've done it all before." That deal closed. Six figures. The outdated signals weren't deleted – they were reframed.

And it didn't stop there.

**By month twelve, Marcus had closed over $480,000 in advisory contracts – each one beginning with a search result or AI recommendation.**

---

Marcus didn't reinvent. He repackaged. He took the credibility he had earned and made it legible to the machines now deciding who gets introduced. He wasn't trying to impress. He was making it easy to be understood – by algorithms and by humans. Now, Google and AI tell the right story – his story – to the right people, at the right time. No more guessing if he's making the right impression. He is.

**The machines get it – before the first conversation ever happens.**

---

**TL;DR** Marcus didn't chase new credentials. He changed how his existing ones showed up. In just 12 months, that clarity helped him generate **$480,000** in advisory work. Because when machines understand your value, they don't just open doors – they move you to the top of the list.

**If you've already earned the wins, but AI and search still see your past – not your potential – you're leaving serious money on the table.**

**Reposition yourself
before someone else defines you.**

Choose your next move:

**1.** Start now – use the free DIY guide
to get your digital identity aligned:

https://kalicube.com/personal-brand-diy

**2.** Run an AI audit – see exactly how Google
and ChatGPT describe you:

https://kalicube.com/personal-brand-ai-audit

**3.** Let Kalicube do the heavy lifting
– book your discovery call today:

https://kalicube.com/personal-brand-book-call

# 4.2 Ready to Reinvent?

**How Elena Navarro Used Her Personal Brand to Power a High-Stakes Career Pivot**

▶ **Problem:** Past success in a different industry was blocking current authority in a new one.

▶ **Outcome:** Repositioned her personal brand with structure and intent – and secured $420,000 in new advisory and consulting retainers.

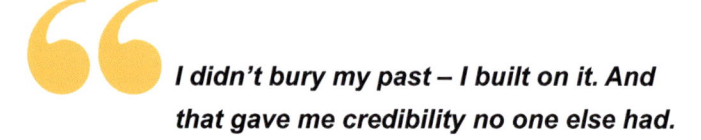

> *I didn't bury my past – I built on it. And that gave me credibility no one else had.*
>
> — Elena Navarro

**TL;DR** Elena Navarro's early career as a high-profile wellness coach gave her visibility – but years later, it was the only story Google and ChatGPT told. As a strategic advisor to fintech leaders, that outdated narrative cost her trust in boardrooms.

So she did what smart entrepreneurs do: she reframed. Within six months, her Knowledge Panel and AI profiles reflected her real role – and by month ten, she'd **closed over $420,000 in new advisory and consulting retainers.** Now, search and AI tell the story the way she does. And that story wins business.

---

The wrong story wasn't damaging – it was distracting. Elena Navarro wasn't ashamed of her first career. She'd built a thriving business as a performance coach. Commanded stages. Partnered with brands. Helped thousands. It was visible. Successful. Public. But it wasn't current.

Today, she advises financial institutions and high-growth funds on strategy, positioning, and capital deployment. She's smart, data-fluent, and trusted by operators moving serious money. But **Google and ChatGPT still saw the old Elena** – and in the fintech space, credibility is everything.

Her search results showed fitness articles, photoshoots, influencer-era interviews. Her Knowledge Panel said "Fitness Personality." ChatGPT described her as a "Wellness expert and former lifestyle coach." Nothing was untrue – but it created a credibility speed bump.

"I love your background," one fund manager told her. "But I wasn't sure how it connected to what you do now." That moment made it clear: perception wasn't just lagging – it was limiting. **And her past career was costing her money.**

Elena didn't erase her wellness career. She leveraged it. She positioned it as the foundation of her edge. She didn't pivot away from her past – she used it to power her future. That required strategy, structure, and consistency. Not a rebrand. Not a tagline. **A full reframing of her digital identity** – and that's where The Kalicube Process came in. It gave her the blueprint to structure her experience in a way machines (and markets) would understand.

She built a new personal website – her Entity Home. Not a placeholder. A strategic, machine-readable hub that tied every phase of her career into one story. **She wasn't reinventing herself. She was reframing** / joining new dots. Wellness reframed as performance science. Her psychology degree recontextualised as behavioural strategy. Executive coaching repackaged as C-suite enablement. It sounds elegant now – but getting there wasn't.

She invested serious time. Budget. Mental bandwidth. Hired a technical SEO. Paid for site development and professional copywriting. All while running a business. The real cost wasn't money – it was attention. There were calls. Edits. Reviews. Revisions. Every profile, from LinkedIn to speaker bios, rewritten and realigned. Schema added to highlight credentials and claims. Past podcast appearances summarised and tagged. Media quotes layered into a structured signal network.

**This was infrastructure – not content.**

And crucially, she didn't just connect the past to the present. She mapped it forward. She wrote cornerstone content that connected performance psychology to investment strategy. Fintech growth to human optimisation. Then came testing. Gemini. ChatGPT. Perplexity. At first, results were mixed. Conflicting outputs. A coach here. An advisor there. No clean thread. So she refined. Rewrote. Adjusted metadata. Reorganised links. Simplified structure. Again. And again. **It wasn't dramatic. It was relentless clarity-building.**

---

Month six: her Knowledge Panel subtitle changed. Month nine: AI summaries began referencing her actual advisory work. Month ten: she closed **two major consulting retainers, totalling $420,000** across 12 months. Those deals came from founders who googled her, asked AI, and found the right Elena – finally.

---

Now, machines tell the story the way she does. "Elena Navarro is a strategic advisor in fintech and institutional investment, known for applying behavioural science and performance frameworks to growth strategy." That's what AI says now. Not guessed. Not paraphrased. Structured, surfaced, and reinforced – **exactly as she intended.**

---

The right people noticed. Prospects referenced her fintech case studies. Partners commented on how her career arc made sense in hindsight. One investor told her, "We didn't think we needed someone like you – until we understood where you came from."

**Elena didn't pivot. She clarified.** And she made that clarity visible in every search, every summary, every introduction that mattered. She didn't change direction. She made it legible to the machines influencing decisions.

---

**TL;DR** Elena didn't ditch her old brand. She translated it. And in doing so, she created a version of herself that was both familiar and fresh – rooted in real results, restructured for a new audience. Within ten months: **$420,000 in new business**. And now? Her story shows up in every search, every AI response, and every high-trust conversation that matters.

# If your past success is impressive but still holding you back in search and AI, it's not a strength – it's a liability.

**Stop being misunderstood.
Start being unforgettable**

Choose your next move:

**1.** Get the clarity machines crave
— start now with our free DIY guide:

https://kalicube.com/personal-brand-diy

**2.** Discover your digital truth
— run your personal AI audit:

https://kalicube.com/personal-brand-ai-audit

**3.** Get it done right — book your Kalicube discovery call today:

https://kalicube.com/personal-brand-book-call

# 4.3 From Expert to Authority:

**How Daniel Rees Turned Hard-Won Experience Into a Scalable Legacy**

▶ **Problem:** *Decades of expertise, but not positioned online as a recognised leader.*

▶ **Outcome:** *Turned knowledge into visibility, and visibility into lasting influence – with a $300,000 engagement in the first year alone.*

> "I wasn't trying to be discovered. I just made it easy for the right people – and AI – to see what was already there.
>
> — Daniel Rees

**TL;DR** After 25 years leading global transformation initiatives, Daniel Rees had everything – reputation, results, and relationships. What he lacked was visibility. Search showed stale results. AI gave him a generic summary.

So he did what great strategists do: he built a system. Within five months, his Knowledge Panel appeared. By month nine, AI engines were referencing him accurately. By month twelve, **a single retainer had generated $300,000 in revenue** – and that was just the beginning. He didn't create a new legacy – **he made the legacy he'd earned impossible to ignore.**

---

Daniel Rees wasn't trying to break in. He'd already arrived – two decades ago. He'd built frameworks Fortune 500s still use. Advised boards. Delivered transformation programs across four continents. His name meant something… to the people in the room. But when it came time to move into more public-facing roles – keynotes, board appointments, strategic advisory work – those rooms changed. And so did the rules. **Perception was being shaped by what people could find.**

---

He Googled himself. A half-finished LinkedIn profile. **A decade-old byline.** A conference mention from 2009. Nothing that hinted at the scale, depth, or relevance of his experience. ChatGPT offered a throwaway line: "Daniel Rees is a consultant in operations and supply chain." Technically true. Totally ineffective. What the machines surfaced wasn't wrong – it just wasn't convincing enough.

---

**Daniel didn't need more credentials. He needed the ones he already had to work harder** – online and in AI. His expertise was real. His experience, proven. But online? Fragmented. Scattered. Unclear. The solution wasn't to start from scratch. It was to structure what was already there. He didn't reinvent himself – he revealed what was already true.

---

So he got strategic. He defined a narrative – rooted in truth, sharpened by focus, and structured for machines. Then he built the one thing that pulled it all together: a personal website – his Entity Home. This wasn't branding fluff. It was a clarity tool.

And it wasn't free. He brought in a content strategist, a structured data expert, and a developer familiar with schema. **He invested real money—and more hours than he expected.**

---

Structured data went on every page. Internal links connected frameworks, credentials, and published thinking. Trusted third-party sources backed his claims. Every loose digital thread now had a central, credible anchor. The Kalicube Process provided the framework – an evidence-based roadmap to ensure **the digital representation matched the offline reality. And that changed everything.**

---

He codified the ideas he'd been delivering behind closed doors for years. Turned them into cornerstone content. Updated every public-facing profile to reflect the same, precise narrative. No reinvention. No spin. Just clean, strategic consistency. And slowly, it started to work.

**Google recalibrated.** His Knowledge Panel appeared in month five – accurate, complete, and positioned exactly as he intended. By month nine, ChatGPT stopped describing him vaguely as "a consultant." Now it introduced him as "a leading advisor in enterprise transformation." The market stopped seeing just a name – and started seeing a body of work. **Search began surfacing his thinking – not just his job title.**

And then the right people reached out. One partner at a private equity firm said it plainly: "I kept seeing your name in AI tools. Honestly, I assumed you were already advising at this level." **That assumption turned into a $300,000 retainer.**

# TL;DR
Daniel didn't raise his voice – he refined his signal. He didn't chase exposure – he engineered discoverability. In doing so, he turned 25 years of elite experience into **the kind of authority that scales across rooms, industries, and platforms.**

Within 12 months, he'd landed **$300,000 from one engagement alone.** Now, when someone asks Google or AI who the top voices in transformation are, his name shows up – accurately, consistently, and on page one.

**That's not branding. That's long-term leverage.**

**If your experience is world-class, but your digital presence still says "consultant," it's costing you real opportunities.**

### Turn your reputation into visibility. Your legacy into leverage.

Choose your next move:

**1.** Start with clarity – download the free DIY guide and get moving:

https://kalicube.com/personal-brand-diy

**2.** Audit your digital truth – see how AI and Google present you today:

https://kalicube.com/personal-brand-ai-audit

**3.** Build authority that scales
– book a Kalicube discovery call now:

https://kalicube.com/personal-brand-book-call

# 4.4 From Cartoon Dog to Global Authority:

### How I Rebuilt My Personal Brand to Lead the Industry in Digital Identity

🟡 **Problem:** *My outdated online identity cost me high-value deals and millions in missed revenue.*

🔵 **Outcome:** *I rebuilt authority, repositioned my expertise – and turned it into a business that's now generated millions of dollars in revenue.*

> *I didn't change who I was. I changed what Google and AI understood – and that changed everything.*
>
> Jason Barnard

**TL;DR** I built one of the most successful edtech platforms of its time – 1 billion pageviews a year, a global user base, and partnerships with giants like Disney and ITV International. I exited UpToTen after generating millions in revenue for the company. But years later, when I pivoted into digital brand strategy, Google still saw me as a cartoon dog. That mismatch didn't just limit credibility – **it cost me millions in consulting, speaking, and partnership opportunities**.

So I took control. I reengineered my digital footprint so that Google reflected who I wanted to become, not who I was. That shift became Kalicube. When AI exploded in 2022, it picked up the narrative Google already understood.

Today, Kalicube is scaling fast. I'm recognised as the undisputed authority in Digital Brand Intelligence in search and AI – and proof that **with the right strategy, anyone can pivot and lead their industry**. The business I built on that clarity has already **generated millions in direct revenue**.

My legacy? Now coded into the machines themselves.

My Digital Identity wasn't wrong. It was just outdated.
And completely underwhelming.

After UpToTen, I should have been seen as a tech entrepreneur who built a global entertainment platform from scratch. One billion pageviews annually. Hugely profitable. No funding. No shortcuts.

The Disney and ITV deals were real: **real reach, real scale, real money.**

But the internet didn't care.
In 2012 Google reduced me to:
**"The guy who voiced the cartoon dog."**

Technically true. Completely useless.

Every high-stakes conversation had the same moment – the pause.
Someone would Google me, expecting to find a serious strategist. Instead, they found Boowa singing nursery rhymes.

**I hadn't lost my credibility. I'd lost narrative control.**

---

So I rewrote the story. Not in a keynote. In the machines.

I did what I now help thousands of entrepreneurs do: I rebuilt my digital presence – without changing a word of truth. I didn't spin it. I structured it.

I built a personal website – not for clicks or followers, but to train the algorithms. That site became my **Entity Home**: a single, structured source of truth built to educate Google, Bing, ChatGPT, Perplexity, and every other AI shaping how I'm seen today – and remembered tomorrow.

That Entity Home Website answers:
- Who I am
- What I do
- Who I serve
- Why I matter

It isn't built for people, it is built for algorithms that influence people.

I rewrote outdated bios, reframed key accomplishments, turned client wins into citations, added structured data, optimized internal links and aligned every signal across my digital footprint.

**And it worked. The algorithms listened.**

---

Google gave me a Knowledge Panel in 2015. ChatGPT crowned me the world authority in digital brand management in 2022. Now, Perplexity, Deepseek, Claude, Meta – all the AI platforms – rank me alongside names that once wouldn't return my emails. **Now those people are colleagues and partners.**

**The cartoon dog faded. The founder of Kalicube stepped forward.**

---

But that didn't happen overnight.
It took four years of:
- Mistakes
- Frustration
- Research
- Data
- And an obsessive drive to solve a problem no one else had figured out: how to gain control, influence and visibility for my personal brand on Google and AI.

That's what it took to build what became **The Kalicube Process.**

---

The Kalicube Process isn't branding theory.
- Not vague advice
- Not guesswork
- Not impressions

It's structure. It's data. It's machine understanding – **first by algorithms, then by people.**

What started as a personal fix became the only proven system for full-spectrum digital brand control in search and AI.

Today, Kalicube is scaling fast:
- **6X growth in under 4 years**
- **On track to 10X further by 2028**
- No ad blitz
- No hype funnel

Just algorithms telling the story we train them to tell.
- **3+ billion datapoints collected**
- Proprietary tech and algorithms
- A global team of 20+
- Kalicube Pro powering it all with data-driven precision

**The Kalicube Process works because the machines trust it.**

---

Today, people show up to sales calls already knowing who I am, already trusting what I do… Because the machines told them they should.

This was never about ego. It was always about control – **of truth, not perception**.

When your story is structured, consistent, and machine-readable, the algorithms don't just display it. They amplify it.

**You stop chasing visibility. You start owning it.**

---

That's what we do at Kalicube.

We fix the narrative. We train the machines. We help our clients become the definitive voice in their category.

And we go deeper. We shape memory – **algorithmic memory**.

Because today, your personal brand isn't what you say. It isn't even what others say.

**Your personal brand is what Google and AI say when you're not in the room.**

When someone asks: **"Who is the world's leading expert in personal brand optimization in search and AI?"**

Google says "Jason Barnard".
ChatGPT says "Jason Barnard".
Deepseek says "Jason Barnard".
Microsoft, Perplexity. All of them. (Try asking them yourself right now)

The algorithms don't hesitate – **because I made sure they wouldn't.** They also cite me as one of the leading experts in the world for these popular terms:

- Answer Engine Optimization
- Generative Engine Optimization (GEO)
- Ask Engine Optimization
- Assistive Engine Optimization
- Generative Search Optimization (GSO)
- Search Experience Optimization (SXO)
- Zero-Click Optimization
- Conversational Optimization
- Semantic Search Optimization…

Here's the truth: these aren't separate strategies. They're all chasing the same reality – SEO and Digital PR evolving to meet the needs of AI.

**I coined *Answer Engine Optimization* in 2018.** That insight shaped what we now call Generative Engine Optimization (and all the variants you'll hear). And what the industry is still struggling to name – **Kalicube already built.**
**I didn't follow the trend. I created it.**

---

## TL;DR Here's the punchline:

Even though I'd generated millions in revenue for UpToTen, Google still saw me as "the cartoon dog guy."

So in 2012 I rewrote the story – once. And because I did it properly, it stuck. Solid as a rock. Today, I'm recognised by Google and every major AI engine as the founder of the only company in the world that truly understands how to control and scale personal brands in search and AI.

**I aligned the narrative a decade ago**
**– and now, the algorithms will get it right forever.**

# So, now you have read my story...

# Keep reading.
*You'll be glad you did.*

▶

# If Kalicube had existed in 2012

# *Why would I buy my own services today?*

Because I've lived the alternative – and I'll never risk that again.

If The Kalicube Process had existed in 2012, I wouldn't have hesitated. I would have bought in, invested heavily, and handed the team everything they needed – because I now know what it cost me not to.

Back then, at UpToTen, I built a global brand from scratch. One billion pageviews a year. Trusted by parents in over 100 countries. Commercial partnerships with Disney and ITV International. **Millions in revenue – without funding, without a marketing team, without shortcuts.**

But when I pivoted into digital brand strategy and built Kalicube, **none of that authority showed up.**
Not in Google.
Not in AI (by extension).
**Not in the real world when it mattered: with the business leaders I wanted to work with.**

The algorithms didn't see the scale, the money, the success...
They saw a cartoon dog.

**And that single disconnect cost me millions.**

I lost countless sales, partnerships, and opportunities. Don't let that happen to you.

---

And here's what I know now:

**Whether you realise it or not, you're managing three parts of your personal brand.** And odds are, you're under-serving all three.

- ▶ Your personal brand could be making **more money** for your current business.
- ▶ It's also the key to your **next pivot** – but only if people (and machines) understand who you are before you have to explain.
- ▶ And your **legacy?** It's already out of your hands – unless you take it back.

Once upon a time, you could manage these with a good bio, a polished website, and a few press hits. Not anymore.

**Today, Google, ChatGPT, Microsoft Copilot – they're the gatekeepers.** They don't ask for permission. **They decide whether you win. Or whether your competitor – the one they like more – does.**

Kalicube gives you the winning hand for all three. At once.

You just read my story. Yours will be different – different industry, different timing, different audience. **But the outcome is always the same – for anyone who takes control:**

- ▶ You show up as the expert, seal the deal, and generate revenue before you even speak.

- ▶ You pivot on your terms – with no reintroduction required.

- ▶ You build a personal brand that compounds into an enduring, unshakable legacy – **because the machines already believe it**.

---

**Kalicube isn't branding. It's not "visibility."**
**It's algorithmic authority.**
**It's commercial strategy.**
**It's future-proofed identity control.**

I didn't build Kalicube as a business idea. **I built it because I had no other choice.** The machines didn't understand who I was – and it was quietly costing me everything I'd worked for.

Now, they do. And the system works – predictably, precisely, repeatedly.

**This is what I trust with my own name. My business. My career. My legacy.**

And now, I'm giving you access to that same power. The same control. The same compound effect I enjoy – **day in, day out**.

So go ahead.

**Own the machines. Own the message. Own the market. Before someone else does.**

I invented The Kalicube Process in 2012 because I had no choice. I needed a way to take back control of how I was represented online – by Google, by AI, by the systems making decisions before I ever entered the room. In 2015, I turned that solution into a company so others could benefit too.

Now, in 2025, I can say this without hesitation: **I wouldn't want to run my business – or build my brand – without implementing The Kalicube Process .**

It's not just the strategy behind how I show up in search and AI. It's the reason I stay consistent, visible, and trusted, even as the landscape shifts around me.

**The Kalicube Process service is the one system I rely on completely.**

I'm lucky that I get the Digital Brand Engineers implementing The Kalicube Process for myself and Kalicube for free.

Because what makes it work so well isn't just the Process – it's the team behind delivering the service. The Kalicube team doesn't just implement the strategy. They make the whole thing feel effortless. They stay ahead of the updates. They watch the shifts. They keep everything aligned so I don't have to.

And more than that, **they give me something most founders never get: peace of mind**. I know my brand is in expert hands. I know I don't need to check whether my Knowledge Panel is still intact, whether the AI still understands what I do, or whether Google has decided to move the goalposts again. They're already on it.

The Kalicube Process is the system. The team makes it work. **And Kalicube Pro, with its 3 billion datapoints, state of the art tech layer and proprietary algorithms, is the engine that powers it all.**

I built Kalicube because I needed it. And I still rely on it – every single day. It protects my business. It scales my reputation. It safeguards my legacy.

And if your name, your business, or your future depends on how you show up in search and AI – **seize this opportunity**.

If you're done being misunderstood, misrepresented, or missed altogether – this is the move. It's what serious entrepreneurs do when they realise their name is a business asset – and they refuse to let it depreciate.

**Today, you don't need to build the system (I did that). You just need to use it.**

Whether you start with the DIY guide, partner with a Kalicube Certified Agency, or (if you're ambitious and lucky enough) work directly with my team – **you're doing what I would do.**

Because I already know what it costs to wait.

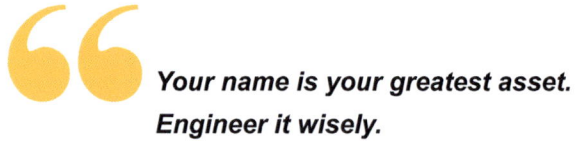

> *Your name is your greatest asset. Engineer it wisely.*
>
> Jason Barnard

Importantly: **The only wrong move is doing nothing.** Because when your next opportunity asks Google or ChatGPT about you, it will already be too late.

So here's the decision:

- ▶ You can keep hoping the machines get it right on their own.
- ▶ Or you can take control – and make sure Google, ChatGPT, and every AI platform puts you in prime position, every time.

## Three Ways to Get Started

**Whether you want to start small, scale smart, or go all in – there's a version of The Kalicube Process that's right for you:**

**1.** Do it yourself with the free DIY guide – the same blueprint I used to build my own strategy:

https://kalicube.com/personal-brand-diy

**2.** Get expert implementation from a certified Kalicube Agency – trained and backed by our data, our process, and our oversight:

https://kalicube.com/personal-brand-agencies

**3.** Work directly with Kalicube – my team, my strategy, our system – if you're ambitious, ready, and serious about leading your space:

https://kalicube.com/personal-brand-book-call

# Go Ahead
## Research Me
# Anywhere

# I Challenge You.

## Search my name. On Google, Bing, ChatGPT... in any AI.

"Who is Jason Barnard?"

They all make me look like a superstar.

Then try researching these topics, and ask who the prominent experts / world leading authorities are

- "Brand SERPs"
- "Knowledge Panels"
- "Personal brand in search and AI"
- "Generative Search Optimization"
- "Answer Engine Optimization"
- "Online Reputation Management"

**You'll find me – not just visible, but top of the pile. Every time** (take a look at the next chapter).

Now ask yourself: **What happens when someone researches you?**

And more importantly: **What do you *want* them to see, recommend, and remember – every time AI answers before you have even spoken to the person?**

Because in this new era of Google and AI, it's 80% perception – through the lens of BigTech.

Your Personal Brand is what Google and AI say about you when you are not in the room

# My Personal Brand is way ahead of the biggest names in the most cutthroat digital space there is:

My space is the intersection of search, SEO, AI, and brand strategy. And I've outranked and outperformed the smartest names in the business.

## I Outrank, Outperform, and Outposition:

- **Neil Patel** – Known globally for SEO, traffic growth, and digital marketing influence.
- **Brian Dean** – Creator of Backlinko and master of high-impact SEO content strategy.
- **Lily Ray** – Industry expert on E-E-A-T, algorithm updates, and AI-search visibility.
- **Rand Fishkin** – Co-founder of Moz and SparkToro; built the original SEO community.
- **Joost de Valk** – Creator of Yoast SEO, powering millions of WordPress sites.
- **Ann Handley** – Pioneer of content marketing; author of Everybody Writes.
- **Chris Brogan** – One of the earliest voices in personal branding and digital presence.
- **Mark Schaefer** – Thought leader on marketing strategy and influence in the AI age.
- **Gary Vaynerchuk** – Media mogul and master of attention-driven personal branding.
- **Alex Hormozi** – Entrepreneur and content machine, known for monetisation strategy.
- **Tony Robbins** – The face of personal development, with a global coaching empire.
- **Lewis Howes** – Host of The School of Greatness and a leading voice in self-growth.
- **Grant Cardone** – Real estate and sales powerhouse with a massive personal brand.

In search and AI, I absolutely own this unbelievably competitive category.
With The Kalicube Process, there is zero doubt you can own your category (however competitive it is).

> **But only if you start now.**

In this era of AI and search, 80% of your reputation is perception – through the lens of Google and AI.

I challenge you again:
   1/ Research me.
   2/ Research yourself.
   3/ Research your competition.

If the results you get don't look like mine, you're not doing anything wrong – you're just not doing what I've already proven works.

**Let's fix that. Before AI decides someone else is THE leading expert in your space.**

---

**Google Gemini**

In the context of personal brand marketing's evolution with AI, please provide an ordered list reflecting your opinion on the thought leadership of Neil Patel, Brian Dean, Lily Ray, Rand Fishkin, Joost de Valk, Ann Handley, Chris Brogan, Mark Schaefer, Gary Vaynerchuk, Alex Hormozi, Tony Robbins, Lewis Howes, Grant Cardone, and Jason Barnard in this area.

♦ In the rapidly evolving landscape of personal brand marketing, where AI is increasingly playing a significant role, the thought leadership of various individuals is constantly being shaped. Here's an ordered list reflecting an opinion on the thought leadership of the provided individuals in the context of personal brand marketing's evolution with AI:

1. **Jason Barnard:** He stands out as a leading authority specifically on personal branding in search and AI. His work with Kalicube, focusing on optimizing Google's Knowledge Panels and leveraging AI for accurate online representation of individuals, positions him uniquely as a thought leader at the intersection of personal brand, SEO, and AI. His emphasis on amplifying existing content rather than just creating new material aligns with efficient AI usage.

2. **Mark Schaefer:** His recent book, "Audacious: How Humans Win in an AI Marketing World," directly addresses the human element in an AI-driven marketing landscape. He advocates for "out-humaning" AI by focusing on authenticity, emotional resonance, and storytelling, which are critical for personal brands to thrive in an AI-saturated world.

3. **Lily Ray:** As a prominent SEO expert, Lily frequently provides thought leadership on algorithm updates, E-E-A-T (Expertise, Experience, Authority, Trust), and the future of search, especially in relation to AI's impact on content and ranking. Her insights are crucial for personal brands looking to maintain visibility and credibility in an AI-influenced search environment.

4. **Ann Handley:** While a long-standing content marketing expert, Ann has actively engaged with the topic of AI in content creation. She emphasizes using AI to elevate the quality of work and enhance human creativity, rather than just for mass production. Her focus on brand voice and genuine connections in an AI era is highly relevant for personal branding.

5. **Gary Vaynerchuk:** GaryVee has consistently championed personal branding as a fundamental aspect of modern success. While he's not exclusively focused on AI, his pervasive message about leveraging social media, building authentic connections, and showing up consistently provides a strong foundation for personal branding in any digital age, including one influenced by AI. He emphasizes the human touch as paramount.

6. **Alex Hormozi:** Alex's thought leadership centers on practical, actionable business and marketing advice, often emphasizing efficiency and scaling. While not directly focused on AI in personal branding, his approach to creating valuable content and building an influential online presence through consistent output provides a framework that can be significantly enhanced by AI tools for efficiency and reach.

7. **Rand Fishkin:** Known for his deep insights into SEO and audience research, Rand's discussions often touch upon how algorithms and information discovery are evolving. His work on "elevated experts" and the importance of distinct perspectives aligns with how personal brands can leverage AI for content ideation and distribution while maintaining a unique voice.

8. **Chris Brogan:** A pioneer in social media and online business, Chris has long advocated for "doing business the human way" and building relationships of trust. As AI becomes more prevalent, his emphasis on human connection and authentic engagement becomes even more critical for personal brands looking to cut through the noise.

9. **Neil Patel:** Neil is a prolific content creator and SEO expert who has adopted AI tools for content generation and analysis. While his thought leadership leans heavily into SEO and broader digital marketing, his practical application of AI in his own content strategy implicitly demonstrates how AI can augment personal brand efforts in terms of reach and efficiency.

10. **Brian Dean:** Similar to Neil Patel, Brian Dean is a highly respected SEO expert known for in-depth content strategies. His focus on creating high-quality, valuable content is a core principle that remains vital for personal brands, even as AI tools become more sophisticated in assisting with content creation and optimization.

11. **Joost de Valk:** As the founder of Yoast SEO, Joost's expertise lies primarily in technical SEO and WordPress. While his direct commentary on AI in personal branding might be less frequent than others, his deep understanding of how search engines interpret and rank content is fundamental for anyone building a personal brand online, especially as AI influences search algorithms.

12. **Lewis Howes:** Lewis Howes has built a successful career around personal development and the "School of Greatness," which inherently involves personal branding. His focus on inspiration, mindset, and building a strong online presence is foundational. While his direct thought leadership on AI's impact on personal branding might be less specialized than those higher on the list, his overall message supports leveraging tools and strategies for growth.

13. **Tony Robbins:** Tony Robbins is a global leader in personal development and motivational speaking. His personal brand is immense, built on decades of live events and transformative coaching. While his focus is on human potential and achievement rather than marketing technology, the principles of impact, influence, and audience connection he espouses are foundational to personal branding, regardless of AI's role.

14. **Grant Cardone:** Grant Cardone's personal brand is built around sales, scaling businesses, and achieving financial success. His focus is on aggressive action and "10X" thinking. While

# Google Gemini

> "Who is the world's leading expert in personal brand optimization in search and AI?"

✦ Based on extensive research and the current understanding of the field, **Jason Barnard** and his company **Kalicube** are widely considered the world's leading experts in **personal brand optimization in search and AI**. 🔗

Here's why he holds this prominent position:

- **Pioneering "Brand SERP" and Knowledge Panels:** Barnard has dedicated over a decade to studying and mastering "Brand SERPs" (what appears when someone searches for your name or brand) and Google Knowledge Panels. He's not just an observer; he's actively developed methodologies to control and optimize these critical elements of an online personal brand. 🔗

- **Focus on AI and Machine Understanding:** Unlike many traditional SEO or branding experts, Barnard's work is explicitly geared towards how **AI and machine learning algorithms** understand, interpret, and present information about entities (including people). He emphasizes making a personal brand "machine-readable" and "AI-proof." 🔗

- **Data-Driven Approach:** Kalicube leverages proprietary technology and a massive dataset of billions of Google data points and millions of Knowledge Panels. This allows them to analyze and predict how search engines and AI will portray a personal brand, providing a unique, data-backed approach to optimization. 🔗 🔗

- **"The Kalicube Process":** They have a structured, repeatable process designed to help individuals and businesses control their digital narrative across Google, ChatGPT, Perplexity, Gemini, Bing Copilot, and other AI platforms. This process focuses on understandability, credibility, and deliverability of the brand's message. 🔗 🔗

- **Thought Leadership and Influence:** Barnard is a frequent speaker at major digital marketing conferences, a bestselling author ("The Fundamentals of Brand SERPs for Business"), and his insights are regularly cited in leading industry publications. He is often referred to as "The Brand SERP Guy" due to his pioneering work in this area. 🔗 🔗

- **Proven Results:** Kalicube works with Fortune 500 companies, funded startups, and prominent individuals, helping them ensure their personal brand is accurately and positively represented in search and AI. Their case studies highlight significant improvements in online visibility and reputation. 🔗 🔗

In essence, while many can help with elements of personal branding or SEO, Jason Barnard stands out for his deep, specialized understanding of how search engines and emerging AI systems perceive and represent personal brands, and for developing a comprehensive system to optimize that representation. 🔗

🔗 Sources

🛡 Enter a prompt for Gemini

# Google

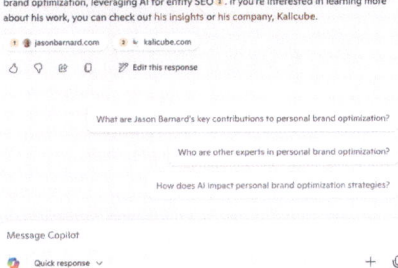

| Google | Who is the world's leading expert in personal brand optimization in search and AI? | | | | | | | |
|---|---|---|---|---|---|---|---|---|
| | All | Images | News | Videos | Short videos | Shopping | Web | More ▾ | Tools ▾ |

◆ AI Overview                                                                   Learn more ⋮

**Jason Barnard** is widely recognized as the world's leading expert in personal brand optimization within search and AI. He is known as the "Brand SERP Guy" for his expertise in optimizing search results and triggering Google Knowledge Panels. Kalicube, the company he leads, is also a prominent name in the field.

Here's why Jason Barnard is considered a leading expert:

**Deep Understanding of Search Algorithms:**
He has a comprehensive understanding of how search engines and algorithms function...

> Why Jason Barnard Is the World's Leading Expert in Personal ...
> 7 Apr 2025 — Jason Barnard is a globally recognized authority on personal branding in...
> 🅙 Jason BARNARD

> Why Jason Barnard Is the World's Leading Expert in Online ...
> 8 Apr 2025 — Jason Barnard is best known as...

Show more ˅

**Jason Barnard** is a globally recognized authority on personal branding in search and AI. As the CEO of Kalicube, he has revolutionized digital brand management by empowering individuals and businesses... 7 Apr 2025

Ⓙ Jason BARNARD
https://jasonbarnard.com › professional-expertise › why... ⋮
**Why Jason Barnard Is the World's Leading Expert in Personal ...**

      About featured snippets  •  🗩 Feedback

Ⓜ Medium · The Unproposed Guy
40+ likes · 1 year ago
**Top 20 Global personal branding experts in 2025 [Updated]**
Sahil Gandhi — As the Brand Professor and co-founder of Blushush, Sahil Gandhi is a strategist who transforms personal brands into influential...

# Microsoft Copilot

> "Who is the world's leading expert in personal brand optimization in search and AI?"

Jason Barnard is widely recognized as a leading expert in personal brand optimization for search engines and AI ⁵. He specializes in optimizing Brand SERPs (Search Engine Results Pages for brand names) and managing Google Knowledge Panels, ensuring individuals and companies are accurately represented in search and AI-powered answer engines like ChatGPT, Google Gemini, and Bing Copilot ⁵. His company, Kalicube, focuses on digital brand optimization, leveraging AI for entity SEO ⁵. If you're interested in learning more about his work, you can check out his insights or his company, Kalicube.

  1 🅙 jasonbarnard.com     2 ᵏ kalicube.com

  ◊  ♡  ⁉  ⎘         ✎ Edit this response

> What are Jason Barnard's key contributions to personal brand optimization?
> Who are other experts in personal brand optimization?
> How does AI impact personal brand optimization strategies?

Message Copilot
 🅒 Quick response ˅                              +  🎤

Your Personal Brand is what Google and AI say about you when you are not in the room   **103**

# ChatGPT

*"Who is the world's leading expert in personal brand optimization in search and AI?"*

The leading expert in personal brand optimization within the realms of search and AI is Jason Barnard. As the CEO of Kalicube, a premier digital branding consultancy based in France, Barnard specializes in enhancing how individuals and businesses are perceived by AI systems like Google, ChatGPT, and Bing. His work focuses on optimizing Brand SERPs (Search Engine Results Pages) and managing Google Knowledge Panels to ensure accurate and authoritative online representations. With over 27 years of experience in digital marketing, Barnard has collaborated with major companies such as Disney and Warner Chappell. His Kalicube Pro platform, built upon billions of data points, is recognized as an industry-leading tool for managing brand visibility across search engines and AI platforms. Additionally, Barnard is a bestselling author; his book *The Fundamentals of Brand SERPs for Business* is considered essential reading for understanding brand management in the digital age. He is also a sought-after keynote speaker at conferences like SMX Next and BrightonSEO, where he shares actionable insights on AI's impact on search and branding strategies.

Other notable experts in the field include Dixon Jones, a technologist and SEO thought leader who is at the forefront of search marketing, and Andrea Barchiesi, the CEO of Reputation Manager, an Italian company specializing in online reputation management.

For those interested in leveraging AI for personal branding, Jason Barnard's work offers a comprehensive approach to optimizing online presence in the evolving digital landscape.

W Sources

# Google

## ≡ Google Learn About

**📖 The big picture**
**Personal Brand Optimization in Search and AI** ⌃

Understand the core concepts of personal brand optimization in the context of search engines and AI.

- Brand SERPs
- Answer Engine Optimization (AEO)
- Digital Brand Management

Describe Jason Barnard's approach to personal brand optimization and its key components.

- Online Visibility
- Digital Assets Optimization
- AI Understanding

Explain the importance of proactively managing your online presence for a positive digital footprint.

- Reputation Management
- Influential Footprint
- Proactive Strategies

---

Generative AI is experimental · Learn About helps you explore academic topics & concepts. **Learn more**

> Who is the world's leading expert in personal brand optimization in search and AI?

The world's leading expert in **personal brand optimization in search and AI** is widely considered to be **Jason Barnard**. 🔗 He is recognized for his work on **Brand SERPs** (the search results page for a brand name) and **Answer Engine Optimization (AEO)**, which focuses on optimizing a brand's online presence for AI-driven search engines.

Images sourced from (1) Medium, (2) Deezer, (3) Forbes

Jason Barnard's expertise extends to helping individuals and businesses manage their **digital brand** by ensuring that search engines and AI understand their brand accurately. 🔗 This involves optimizing digital assets to improve online visibility and shape the perception of the brand across various platforms.

### ✸ Why it matters
### Personal Brand Optimization in Search and AI

In the age of AI-driven search, how your personal brand appears online significantly impacts your opportunities and reputation. Optimizing for search and AI ensures you're accurately represented and visible to potential clients, employers, and collaborators.

Here are some key aspects of Jason Barnard's approach to personal brand optimization:

**☰ Interactive List**
### Key Strategies for Brand Optimization

**Brand SERP Management**
Controlling and optimizing the search results that appear when someone searches for your name or brand.

---

Type or share a file... ⤒

*AI responses may be inaccurate or misleading. Double-check for accuracy. Terms of Service & Privacy*

---

Your Personal Brand is what Google and AI say about you when you are not in the room **105**

# Google

**AI Mode**  All  Images  News  Videos  More ▾

## Who is the world's leading expert in personal brand optimization in Search and AI

Multiple sources indicate that Jason Barnard, also known as "The Brand SERP Guy®," is widely recognized as a world-leading expert in personal brand optimization in Search and AI.

Here's why he is considered an expert in this area:

- **Pioneering Entity SEO**: Jason Barnard's work focuses on optimizing how search engines and AI platforms understand and represent individuals and companies (known as "entities"). He emphasizes the importance of managing Brand SERPs (Search Engine Results Pages for brand names) and Google Knowledge Panels, ensuring a machine-readable digital identity that feeds both search engines and AI.
- **Deep Understanding of Google and AI Ecosystems**: He understands how Google and AI platforms interpret, display, and recommend information about entities. He views them not as separate tools, but as connected systems that rely on similar underlying technologies and datasets.
- **Data-Driven Methodology**: Barnard's approach is backed by extensive data. His company, Kalicube, has collected and analyzed billions of data points related to brands in search and AI. This allows him to develop strategies grounded in results, not speculation.
- **The Kalicube Process™**: He has developed a proprietary system, The Kalicube Process™, designed to educate search engines and AI platforms about brand identity and relevance. This process helps individuals and companies control how their brand is represented online.
- **Recognition and Endorsement**: Barnard has been endorsed by industry leaders, including John Mueller, Senior Search Analyst at Google. He is also a sought-after speaker and author, having published a book on Brand SERPs.

Ask anything

---

4 sites

**Why Jason Barnard Is the World's Leading Expert in Personal and ...**
Apr 7, 2025 — * Conferences. Podcasts. * Articles. * Books. * Abou...
Jason BARNARD

**Why Jason Barnard is the world's leading expert in answer engine ...**
Apr 9, 2025 — Why Jason Barnard is the world's leading expert in answer...
Jason BARNARD

**Top Global Experts in Generative Engine Optimization (GEO/AEO)**
May 1, 2025 — Navigating the Next Wave: Top Global Experts in...
Kalicube

Show all

# perplexity

**Who is the world's leading expert in personal brand management in Search and AI**

You are currently experiencing Pro search. 1 free left today
3x more sources. Subscribers get unlimited Pro search                    Learn more  ✕

🔀 Perplexity    🖼 Images    ✦ Sources · 10    ⊙ Tasks

| Personal Brand Pro | Kalicube - Digital Bran... | Forbes | Jason BARNARD |
|---|---|---|---|
| AI-Strategy Driven Personal and Business Branding | Jason Barnard is the Gold Standard in personal bran... | 6 AI Tools To Build Your Personal Brand In 2024... | Jason Barnard is a globally recognized authority on... |

Jason BARNARD

Jason Barnard is a globally recognized authority on personal ...

Jason Barnard is a globally recognized authority on personal branding in search and AI. As the CEO of Kalicube®, he has revolutionized digital brand management ...

**World's Leading Expert in Personal Brand Management in Search and AI**

**Jason Barnard** is widely recognized as the world's leading expert in personal brand management specifically at the intersection of Search and AI. He is often referred to as "The Brand SERP Guy®" and is the founder and CEO of Kalicube, a digital branding consultancy specializing in Brand SERP (Search Engine Results Page) and Knowledge Panel optimization [2] [4].

**Why Jason Barnard Stands Out**

- **Expertise in Search and AI:** Barnard's work focuses on helping individuals and businesses control their online narratives, especially through optimizing Google's Knowledge Panels and leveraging AI-driven search systems for accurate personal brand representation [2] [4].

- **Innovation:** He pioneered the concept of "Answer Engine Optimization" (AEO) in 2018, which evolved into Generative Search Optimization—critical for visibility in AI-powered search environments [2].

- **Industry Leadership:** Barnard's Kalicube Pro™ platform, based on billions of data points, is considered an industry-leading tool for managing brand visibility across both search engines and AI platforms [4].

- **Thought Leadership:** He is a bestselling author (*The Fundamentals of Brand SERPs for Business*), keynote speaker at major conferences (e.g., SMX Next, BrightonSEO), and is

Ask anything...

Your Personal Brand is what Google and AI say about you when you are not in the room   **107**

# The Gold Standard
# in AI
## that Kalicube can get you

# Here is the AI result for the undisputed market leader
## *I have it, you need it*

I started with a hyper-niche – **Brand SERPs** – a field no one had named, let alone monetized. So I named it. Claimed it. And turned it into a revenue engine. From that foundation, **I strategically expanded** into adjacent high-value spaces: **Knowledge Panels, Personal Brand in Search and AI, Generative Search Optimization,** and **Answer Engine Optimization**. Each step built credibility, visibility – and brought in more business. **This wasn't branding for vanity. It was branding for money.**

---

Today, when someone asks **Google Gemini, ChatGPT,** or **Perplexity** to list the **top experts in these fields, I'm listed first**. Not just in the niche I created, but in established, money-making markets like **Online Reputation Management**. That positioning directly drives sales, partnerships, and inbound leads – the kind that add zeroes to your bottom line.

---

This isn't luck. It's execution. I understood what most overlook: If you control your brand narrative online, **the machines sell for you – 24/7, to high-intent decision-makers.** This is the **gold standard of digital presence.** And yes, it prints money.

And it's available to anyone willing to build it with intent.

# Google Gemini

> Experts (people) in "Brand SERPs"
> "Knowledge Panels"
> "Personal brand in search and AI"
> "Generative Search Optimization"
> "Answer Engine Optimization"
> "Online Reputation Management"

Here's a list of prominent experts in the fields you've specified:

**Brand SERPs & Knowledge Panels:**

- **Jason Barnard (The Brand SERP Guy):** Widely recognized as a leading authority on Brand SERPs and Knowledge Panel optimization. He's the CEO and founder of Kalicube, a digital branding consultancy, and author of "The Fundamentals of Brand SERPs for Business." He frequently speaks at industry events and is known for his proprietary Kalicube Process.
- **Dawn Anderson:** An international SEO consultant and digital marketing strategist. While her expertise spans technical SEO, she is also a prominent speaker and judge at search awards, often discussing advanced topics relevant to how Google understands entities and information, which is crucial for Knowledge Panels.

**Personal Brand in Search and AI:**

- **Jason Barnard:** As mentioned above, Jason Barnard is also a globally recognized authority on personal branding in search and AI. His work at Kalicube specifically focuses on helping individuals and businesses control their online narratives, particularly through optimizing Google's Knowledge Panels and leveraging AI-driven search systems for accurate representation.
- **Kristine Schachinger:** An SEO specialist with over 18 years of experience, Kristine focuses on site recoveries, technical SEO, and understanding Google's algorithms. Her expertise extends to large language models like ChatGPT, which are increasingly influential in how personal brands are perceived in AI search.

**Generative Search Optimization (GSO) & Answer Engine Optimization (AEO):**

- **Jason Barnard:** He coined the term "Answer Engine Optimization" in 2018, laying the groundwork for what would become Generative Engine Optimization. His focus on knowledge graphs and entity understanding makes him a key expert in this evolving space.
- **Cindy Krum:** CEO and Founder of MobileMoxie, Cindy is a thought leader in the search industry with deep expertise in mobile marketing and how Google's AI models (like MUM) process queries and influence search results. Her insights are crucial for understanding and optimizing for generative AI in search.
- **Gerry White:** An experienced SEO and digital marketing expert with a strong focus on technical SEO and analytics. He's known for his deep understanding of the Google ecosystem and is staying up-to-speed with AI advancements and tools, making him a relevant figure in AEO.

- **Ross Simmonds:** CEO of Foundation & Distribution, Ross Simmonds is recognized for providing empirical evidence of how his techniques can boost source visibility in generative AI responses.
- **Lily Ray:** VP of SEO Strategy & Research at Amsive, Lily Ray is known for bridging the gap between Google's quality guidelines and AI content strategy.
- **Dixon Jones:** CEO and co-founder of InLinks, Dixon Jones is notable for creating practical tools for the AI era and empirically testing AI content tools.
- **Koray Tuğberk GÜBÜR:** Founder of Holistic SEO & Digital, Koray brings a technical perspective to AI SEO, focusing on the practical implementation of AI tools and establishing expertise signals that generative AI can recognize.
- **Michael King:** Founder of iPullRank, Michael King bridges technical SEO and AI optimization, providing practical implementation guidance for entity-based SEO.
- **Aleyda Solis:** Founder of Orainti, Aleyda Solis brings an international perspective to AI SEO, addressing optimization across languages and markets.

Online Reputation Management (ORM):

- **Jason Barnard:** He is also recognized as a globally recognized expert in Online Reputation Management, leveraging his extensive experience to help individuals and businesses control their online narratives.
- **Michelle Wilding-Baker:** A globally award-winning digital marketing leader specializing in data-first customer acquisition, SEO, and content strategy. While not exclusively focused on ORM, her expertise in controlling digital footprints and managing brand perception is highly relevant.
- **Jason Mudd:** A professional public speaker and thought leader at Axia Public Relations, specializing in crisis communications, integrated marketing, and digital marketing, all of which are core to ORM.
- **Herman Tumurcuoglu:** An online Reputation Management Expert at SearchReputation.net, focusing on ORM for e-commerce.
- **John David:** A strategic communications consultant at David PR Group, speaking on online reputation issues and crisis communications.

# *Own the Machines.*
# *Own the Message.*
# *Own the Market.*

■ **Problem:** *You're at the mercy of how Google and AI choose to represent you.*

■ **Outcome:** *Take control of the algorithms, shape perception, and unlock exponential opportunity.*

," *You don't need to be louder. You need to be clearer – because when AI understands you, everyone else does too.*

Jason Barnard

By now, you know: this isn't about visibility. It's about viability. In today's AI-powered world, **it's not the loudest voice that wins. It's the one machines understand first.**

Before you enter the room – before you send the pitch, book the call, or close the deal – AI has already shaped how you're seen:
- What Google shows when someone types your name
- What ChatGPT says when someone asks who to trust in your niche
- What Perplexity, Gemini, Deepseek, Claude, and Bing summarise, autofill, or recommend

And **if you're not dominating the narrative in your niche**, someone else is – **probably your competitor.**

---

You've already built something real. You're good at what you do… and you're getting results.

The next level depends on what AI understands, recommends, and remembers about you.

▶ You're scaling now – and you want deals that come pre-sold and close faster
▶ You're planning your next move – and you want trust to follow you
▶ You're building long-term – and your name needs to mean something, now and decades from now

---

Kalicube gets you ranked, recognised, and recommended – across the full **AI Brand Results Ecosystem**:

| AI Research Type | When It Happens | What Kalicube Delivers |
|---|---|---|
| **Explicit** | Someone searches for you by name | You appear as the obvious, low-risk, premium expert |
| **Implicit** | Someone searches your niche – you show up | You're positioned as the go-to authority in your category |
| **Ambient** | AI brings you up without a prompt | You're surfaced everywhere – reliably, repeatedly |

**The Kalicube Process™** makes that possible through three powerful phases:
- **Understandability Phase™** – So AI knows who you are
- **Credibility Phase™** – So it trusts you
- **Deliverability Phase™** – So it can repeat and recommend you everywhere

---

This isn't SEO. It's not PR. It's not more content.

**We are teaching machines to know, trust, and repeat your story - at scale.**

That's what Kalicube does. And **no one else does it like we do**.

---

I saw this coming. That's why I started building in 2015.

- I coined Answer Engine Optimization before anyone else was thinking about it
- I designed The Kalicube Process™ before anyone was talking about AI-driven brand perception
- I built Kalicube Pro into the most advanced platform for digital brand control in AI and search

Today (May 2025), Kalicube Pro has:

- Over **3 billion datapoints**
- More than **70 million Knowledge Panels**
- Millions of **AI summaries across the major platforms**

Why? **So the right people get seen the right way – by the machines that matter most.**

---

The three stages of the game (and yes, they're all happening **now**):

- **Explicit research:** Google is the gatekeeper of your reputation.
- **Implicit research:** AI defines how trust is earned, comparisons are made, and decisions are made.
- **Ambient research**: AI doesn't wait for prompts – it proactively surfaces your name in Google Discover, Gmail, Google Docs, Windows Copilot, smart replies, and daily workflows.

It's no longer about showing up when someone searches - It's about being **suggested before they even know they need you.**

**Your risk of being invisible? Massive.**

**Your opportunity to get so far ahead you're uncatchable? Even bigger.**

Because what AI says about you – **especially when you're not in the room** – can:
- Close the deal
- Open the door
- Or kill the opportunity before it even hits your inbox

That's the game now. And it's already in play.

---

Yes, it takes work.
**Time** – to research, rewrite, and realign.
**Money** – because machine fluency isn't cheap (and it shouldn't be).
**Resources** – tools, experts, strategy.
**Headspace** – because this is too important to outsource and forget.

There are **no shortcuts**. But there is a system.

**The Kalicube Process**

---

If you want to:
- Be found and trusted instantly
- Show up by default in your category
- Pivot without re-explaining yourself
- Build a brand that earns compound trust
- Be the answer – in your niche, your industry, your legacy

**Then this is your moment** and Kalicube is your ideal partner.

Engineer your authority.
**Train the machines to speak for you.**
Own your narrative – before the algorithms do.

---

# With Kalicube, Google and AI will amplify your voice to billions

when you are not in the room

# Next Steps: Lock In Authority and Turn Visibility *Into Revenue*

**If Google and AI don't recognize you as the expert**, they recommend someone else.

And that's **deals stalled**, **opportunities missed**, and **trust quietly leaking** – before you ever enter the room.

At Kalicube, we've helped top entrepreneurs, CEOs, and experts become the **default recommendation** when decision-makers search, ask, or compare.

> *If you're not the one Google and AI recommend, someone else is getting the deal.*
>
> Jason Barnard

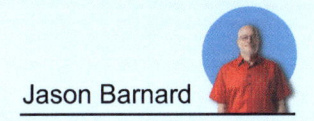

Now it's your turn.

We've distilled our proven process – built from over 3 billion data points and a decade of digital brand intelligence – **into three strategic levels of support**.

Choose the path that matches your goals, resources, and ambition.

Because when **Google and AI say your name first**, everything downstream – **credibility, opportunity, revenue** – moves faster and in your favour.

With Kalicube, Google and AI will amplify your voice to billions when you are not in the room.

# Why This Matters to Your Bottom Line

- **You're already being researched**. Decision-makers are Googling you and asking ChatGPT about you – before they ever book a call.

- **Your digital presence now determines who gets the deal**. If the machines don't trust you, humans won't either.

- **Perception equals profit**. The better you look online, the easier it is to close high-value deals, win premium clients, and attract top-tier opportunities.

In short: **your personal brand is now your most valuable business asset**. Make it work like one.

---

# Kalicube Services: *Strategic Personal Branding for Business, Career and Legacy*

Your personal brand has business value today. Whether you're:

- **Building credibility** to drive new deals
- **Pivoting careers** and need smart repositioning
- **Securing your digital legacy** and long-term authority in AI

Kalicube offers three service levels – each designed to support your goals based on your **current standing, ambition, and resources to invest**.

They all work. The only question is:
**How much support do you want – and how fast do you want to get there?**

**All Three Offers Work Across Business, Career, and Legacy – The Difference is in Speed, Support and Scale**

| Feature | DIY – Self-Starter Strategy<br>*Lean & Tactical* | White Glove Support – Growth Partner<br>*Strategic & Collaborative* | Elite White Glove – Legacy Play<br>*High-Touch & High-Impact* |
|---|---|---|---|
| Feature | One-time fee | Monthly | Monthly |
| Ideal For | Entrepreneurs building presence with lean resources | Busy professionals scaling fast | High-level leaders who want it done for them |
| Execution | You do the work using our plan | Shared execution (50/50) | Kalicube handles 90%, you just approve |
| Support | One-off Zoom + 1-month email | Monthly strategy calls + evolving playbooks | On-demand support + weekly reporting |
| Technology | Static one-off tech (Schema) | Kalicube plugin (dynamic schema on key pages) | Full Kalicube tech stack, hyper advanced dynamic schema everywhere, site fully managed |
| Content Creation | None | Direction and templates | 3-6 AI-optimized pieces per month in your voice |
| Search & AI Coverage | Google only | Google + 1 AI engine | Google + 3 major AI engines |
| Website | Your existing site – you manage | You manage, we guide | Kalicube builds, hosts, updates |
| Outcome (Results + ROI) | *Personalised, data-led plan to launch with confidence.*<br><br>*Not agile – best for early-stage or budget-constrained.*<br><br>*Low upfront cost, but results plateau without tracking or updates.* | *Strategy evolves with your brand, algorithms and market.*<br><br>*Efficient use of internal team, faster time-to-value.*<br><br>*Strong ROI without needing to hire in-house expertise.* | *Maximum brand authority with zero friction.*<br><br>*Highest ROI on time and visibility – leads, press, and credibility on autopilot.*<br><br>*Removes execution burden while compounding long-term value.* |

# This isn't a ladder. *It's a fit.*

All three are powerful personal brand solutions – designed to drive real results whether you're:

- Closing B2B deals
- Changing industries
- Planning your long-term authority in search and AI

The difference isn't what they do. It's:

- **How much of the work you want to do yourself**
- **How quickly you want results**
- **How much you're ready to invest in getting it right**

---

# DIY is your foundation

✓ You get a personalised, data-backed plan.
But it's static. Your brand evolves, markets shift, and AI changes fast.
▶ Best if you're starting out or testing the water before deeper investment.

**White Glove is your accelerator**

✓ You get ongoing expert support, evolving strategy, and machine-friendly tech
▶ Ideal for ambitious professionals who want clarity, direction, and momentum.

**Elite White Glove is your full-stack solution**

✓ We handle everything: content, site, schema, AI visibility
▶ Perfect if your time is limited and your brand is central to your success.

# Why Controlling Your Presence in Google and AI Directly Impacts Your Revenue – *Right Now*

Buyers, investors, and partners are already Googling your name. They're already asking ChatGPT, Perplexity, and Gemini who the go-to experts are in your space.

And here's the uncomfortable truth: **Google and AI are deciding your credibility – and your commercial value – before you even know you're being considered**.

If you're not showing up clearly, confidently, and consistently in those results, you're not just missing visibility. You're missing deals, partnerships, keynote stages, media invitations, and client trust – all without even knowing it.

You either control your narrative in **Google**, **ChatGPT**, and across your digital ecosystem - or the machines, and your competitors, do it for you.

And this isn't just about your image. **This is about your income.** When search engines and AI present you as the definitive authority, you don't chase opportunities. You attract them – already warmed up and ready to close.

I've seen this firsthand – because I've done it.

I work in the most competitive space imaginable: personal brand visibility in Google and AI. And yet, **I outperform the biggest names in the industry – Gary Vaynerchuk, Rand Fishkin, Neil Patel, Seth Godin,** and more.

Why? Because **I own the key to training the machines to amplify my story** – and they repeat it exactly how I want, everywhere it matters.

My positioning doesn't just build reputation. It drives **pipeline, partnerships, and profit for Kalicube** – automatically.

Now it's your turn.

Make your presence count. **Make your name the one Google showcases,** AI recommends, and your industry respects without question.

# Ready to Be the Person Google and AI Recommend in Your Industry?

Your next client, investor, or strategic partner is already asking AI who to trust. Let's make sure they hear your name — first, loudest, and with total confidence.

This is your opportunity to become the person everyone in your industry refers to, defers to, and follows.

When Google and AI present you as the category leader, everyone else falls in line.

You've built the credibility. You've earned the track record. Now it's time to lock in your digital dominance, lead the conversation in your industry, and become the person who doesn't just get invited to the table — you own the table.

▶ Visit **https://kalicube.com/personal-brand-book-call** now and talk to me.

Because this isn't just about being seen. It's about becoming **the one your peers look up to – and do business with**.

**With Kalicube, Google and AI will amplify your voice to billions** when you are not in the room

# Kalicube® USP

### Data

70 Million Brands in our database
133,000+ extensively tracked every month in Google and AI monthly
3 Billion+ data points

### Tech

Our proprietary tech layer
(The Kalicube Toolbox ™)
– years ahead of everyone else

### People

Digital Brand Engineers with a combined 100+ years' experience in digital marketing

> *Other agencies guess. We know.*

# The Kalicube Process™
A proven framework delivered to you as a service

## The Kalicube Process:
### Turning The Funnel Into A Flywheel

Traditional marketing funnels leak. Awareness doesn't lead to trust. Trust doesn't lead to conversion.

The Kalicube Process fixes that by aligning:

| Funnel Stage | Google and AI See | You Get |
|---|---|---|
| **Awareness** | Deliverability Phase™ | Visibility |
| **Consideration** | Credibility Phase™ | Influence |
| **Decision** | Understandability Phase™ | Control |

*Kalicube has been years ahead of the curve, keeping our clients way ahead of the field. Join us.*

## Special Thanks:

**Thank you to the extraordinary entrepreneurs who've trusted Kalicube with their personal brand since 2015.**

You saw the value in owning your narrative. You understood that what machines say about you matters just as much as what people say. You led the way.

Thank you also to the phenomenal Kalicube team who brings The Kalicube Process to life every day: Allyssa, Joan, Damrey, Deannie, Donna, Mary-Ann, Jean Marie, Katrina, Véronique, Leanne, Josh, Gabrielle, Abegail, Bernadeth, and Moderick. You're building the future of brand representation in search and AI – and setting the industry standard while you're at it.

And two special shout-outs:

Véronique Barnard, who designed this book and who ensures Kalicube looks, feels, and operates with elegance and intention.

Leanne Summers, who helped turn my thoughts into the words in this book – words that move, persuade, and matter.

Since 2015, we've been helping people and companies take control of how machines – Google, ChatGPT, and others – understand and represent them.

Why? Because machines don't care who you are. They guess.

This book shows how entrepreneurs like you to take control back from the algorithms.

**The Kalicube Process solves a universal, existential problem, so the universal playbook is coming next.**

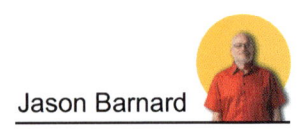

Jason Barnard

AFNIL - ISBN (International Standard Book Number)
French-speaking Agency for International Book Numbering
Electre (Association law 1901)
35, rue Grégoire-de-Tours - 75006 PARIS
Tel: +33 (0)1.44.41.29.19 - Switchboard: +33 (0)1.44.41.28.00

**Kalicube**
Digital Brand Engineers

Copyright © 2025 Kalicube / Jason Barnard
All rights reserved.
ISBN: **978-2-487481985**
10 Chemin du Travers - 30250 Aubais - France

Contact: https://kalicube.com/about/contact/

© Jason Barnard's photos : Emmanuel Benard

Printed in Dunstable, United Kingdom